THE

Thoroughly Modern

Married Girl

Broadway Books

New York

THE

Thoroughly Modern
Married Girl

Staying Sensational After Saying "I Do"

Sara Bliss

BROADWAY

PRINTED IN THE UNITED STATES OF AMERICA

BROADWAY BOOKS and its logo, a letter B bisected on the diagonal, are trademarks of Broadway Books, a division of Random House, Inc.

Visit our website at www.broadwaybooks.com

First edition published 2003

Cover and inside illustrations by Monica Lind

Library of Congress Cataloging-in-Publication Data

Bliss, Sara.
The thoroughly modern married girl : staying sensational after saying "I do" / by Sara Bliss.—1st ed.
p. cm.
1. Marriage. 2. Married women—Conduct of life. I. Title.

HQ734 .B655 2003
306.81—dc21
2002028380

ISBN 0-7679-1370-1

1   3   5   7   9   10   8   6   4   2

For Brooks

Contents

Introduction

The Honeymoon Is Over? What Now?

So you're the star of the best date movie ever. One minute you're Miss Sensational Single Girl, the next minute you saw Him and you knew your single days were numbered. You prevented your gorgeous and brainy friends from getting to him before you could. You batted those long eyelashes of yours and happily handed over your digits. You lost your act. Your copy of *The Rules* was tossed out the window. If he had a girlfriend at the time, she was quickly eliminated. He actually called when he said he would! He even showed up on time. He didn't necessarily resemble that husband checklist you had in your head. But he was even funnier, sweeter, and groovier than your fantasy Prince Charming.

He grew on you. Love blossomed. People in your office kept asking what you were smiling at. He used "we" in the future tense. He said the *L* word. You said it back. You finally understood what all the fuss is about. You became each other's biggest fans. Maybe a few bumps were encountered along the way. OK, perhaps they were craters, but you came out swinging. Ultimately you invaded his heart and there was nowhere to run. He suggested you become lifetime roommates. "What's marriage but a piece of paper?" Your Guy asked. You weren't keen on shacking up. He spent a night or two alone and determined that an evening without you wasn't nearly as fun as one together. The only right choice was to make you his bride. Your Guy marched into a jewelry store or the family vault and picked out the right rock. He popped the question. You acted like you were totally surprised and hadn't been waiting since day one. Just one little word from you, "Oui! Si! Yes! Absolutely!" and your life would change completely. After a whirlwind of showers, parties, and tearful or giggly "I do's," you're hitched! You want to high-five the gods of love.

So what now? You've played the ultimate dating game and won. What's next? Perfect life, little house, a couple of dogs, maybe a baby or three? No more worrying about the relationship, right? Not so fast. This is normally where the date movie ends, so it's not your fault you don't really know what to expect. The whole time you were dating, you focused on making him yours and then making sure he was "the one." Throughout your engagement you were concentrating on hot pink or pale pink for your bridesmaids (maybe both?), whether your band should play the Macarena (Not!), and practicing your first kiss as man and wife (chaste peck or full-on Al and Tipper?).

But now that you're married, the fun really starts, girls. If you thought you knew him inside and out, that you're more in love than you could ever be, you're wrong. The fact is, life together gets better . . . and more complicated. Never fear, I've been there and so have countless other Married Girls who filled me in on their transition from sassy single to savvy married. I've gathered their tales of love, lust, and learning how to live with their men, to give you the skinny on married life. This isn't a primer for having a perfect marriage (no such thing, honey), but a handbook to help you navigate the wonderful world of wedlock with a modern perspective and a little finesse. So read on, I'm here to let you in on what to really expect, how to handle the flat tires on the road of lifetime love, and how to salsa into the other dimension of being a Thoroughly Modern Married Girl.

Who Is the Thoroughly Modern Married Girl?

As a Thoroughly Modern Married Girl you waited till the right man came along, and even then took your time to be absolutely certain he was worth the long trip down the aisle. What was the hurry? You were a Sensational Single Girl, you were Fabulous, you were Swell, you were a Bad Girl on the Open Road. You didn't need Prince Charming to rescue you. You just wanted a soulmate. And after a lengthy and oftentimes exhausting quest, you've found the guy who's lucky enough to spend the rest of his days by your side.

So what's a hip single girl to do in the seemingly traditional world of wedlock? Enter the Thoroughly Modern Married Girl. You flout conventional concepts of marriage. You two started by writing your own vows and now you're writing your own rules. You take only the traditional concepts of marriage you vibe with (changing your name so you're a team) and adopt some modern ones as well (you might bring home the bacon and he may fry it up in a pan). You and Your Guy are a team, making decisions based on what's best for you as a pair. Whatever works for you, you say. You're creating your own personal definition of marriage where you're copilots, steering your course together and handing the controls to each other when necessary.

Now that you're hitched, you know *some* things will change, but you're *not* going to change who you are. You're not going to start living through your man and stop going to yoga class, dishing on the phone with your sister, and writing your screenplay. Whatever makes you the person he fell for in the first place, you'll keep on doing. Same goes for him. You have always been about friends and family and you didn't drop everyone in your life when your prince rode up. You're still there to take your friends for a spin and a little retail therapy when they're feeling blue, as well as providing a little love therapy when Your Guy's had a bad day. You'll keep on being a chic, independent, clever, successful babe even after you've got the ring on your finger. There's nothing matronly about matrimony for you.

You put a lot of effort into making your single life fabulous, and you're not going to just sit around and watch cable, feeling "settled." As a Thoroughly Modern Married Girl you're going to put just as much effort into making married life marvelous. You may have tossed your little black book on your way to the altar, but you're absolutely going to hang on to your little black dress.

Leaving Singledom Behind

So maybe you're wondering what will change now that you've crossed over the threshold to become a Married Girl (aka an MG)? Well, you spent years (not to mention many tubes of lipstick) carefully cultivating the alluring single girl persona that stopped Mr.

Right dead in his tracks. Cleavage was exposed (if you have it, flaunt it). You even learned to do Wild Turkey shots, shoot a wild pheasant, and rope steer with the boys (you had to prove you weren't a wimpy girl). Getting a cute guy to ask you out? No problem. You had him over in three easy steps without ever seeming like you were picking him up. Dateless at a wedding? No moping in the corner, you were on the dance floor all night boogying with bachelors A, B, and C.

After all that professional dating, you finally met Mr. Right and it's time to kiss singledom goodbye. While it's a thrilling moment when you realize you won't have to kiss any more frogs, you're going to have to make a few adjustments to move smoothly from Miss to Mrs. (well, Ms. to Ms.) All the sassy single girl skills you've spent years perfecting just don't apply in a Married Girl's world. After spending your entire dating life trying to figure out how to attract men, now that you've mastered the art you have to stop. No more "look at me" stunts like dancing on bars. While your husband may think it's cool for him at home (on the coffee table), chances are he won't be too psyched if you decide to shake a tail feather in front of a roomful of men. And the single guy radar that you developed to home in on available guys should be put to use in setting up your best friend. Out dancing with your single girlfriends? If a handsome bachelor approaches you, just point him in the direction of your favorite single gal pal. Still have your little black book? Pass it on.

Living Married

Part of leaving your single days behind means adjusting to the fact that you now share a space, perhaps a very small space, with the love of your life. After you move in with Your Guy, you will need to make a few changes to your daily routine. While certain habits may have been perfectly acceptable when you lived on your own, they might be horrifying to your live-in love. No more throwing your clothes all over the bedroom while trying on every outfit you own before going out. Your Guy just might want to see the floor as he walks on it. Nights spent eating M&M's and popcorn in bed, weeping hysterically over *Terms of Endearment* or *Steel Magnolias* will now be carefully orchestrated events shared with other female friends. Chances are, he won't want to join you in your cinematherapy. Your weekly beauty nights when you sleep with your hands in heated gloves, face covered in a green pore-cleaning mask, hair in rollers, body covered in greasy deep-moisturizing treatment might not be appreciated by the man you now share your bed with. Living off Diet Coke, cereal, tuna fish, and white wine may have worked for you and your always dieting roommates, but chances are Your Guy will want to eat a meal every once in a while. You may have to put things that you would never consume, like beef jerky or vegetable juice, in your kitchen depending on Your Guy's culinary taste. Letting the dog eat off your plate and other secret behavior you developed when no one was looking should be kept secret, even from your husband. You want Your Guy to understand who you really are. You don't want to gross him out.

On the other hand, there are multiple benefits to being married and living together. When you have an argument you no longer have to worry about breaking up. You're in it for the long haul. When you're dancing to Aretha Franklin before getting ready for a party, you have a dance partner other than your dog. When you forget burgers on burger night you now have someone who can pick up some patties on his way home. The nights your girlfriends call you crying after some handsome but horrible single man made them blue, you can now offer them Your Guy's sensible opinion on what on earth to do. You finally have proof that there are guys out there (and, happily, in your apartment) who don't have panic attacks at the first sign of commitment. You can throw away your dog-eared copies of *Stupid Things We Do for Love, More Stupid Things We Do for Love*, and *Successful and Alone*, books you bought when your love life wasn't as stellar as it is today. Leaks, electric outages, and flat tires can now be fixed and heavy furniture moved without paying anyone or having to do it yourself. (I know you're not a helpless woman and can do it on your own, but if you don't have to, why?) If you're extraordinarily lucky Your Guy likes to cook and will whip up two eggs over easy and a smoothie and bring them to you in bed along with a copy of the *New York Times* style section. Heaven on a Sunday morning. Regular smooching is also part of the deal. No more kissing your dog on New Year's. No more wondering if your date is going to kiss you goodnight. Your Guy is there to smooch every day. What could be better than that?

For Better or Worse

Now that you're married you probably thought that at the very least your frantic obsessing about relationships and men would be over. You figured you two would never argue again and "happily ever after" meant a lifetime of ultimate perfection? You thought that feeling lonely and bummed out were only a symptom of the angst that breakups and looking for love can bring? Well, not exactly. Just to remind you, there was a "worse" in those vows you took and every once in a while "worse" will pop up like an ugly weed.

You have a new set of obstacles to navigate now that you're hitched. You have to figure out how to be as crazy about each other as when you first met despite having to negotiate finances, debate who cooks dinner, and cope with a second set of nagging parents. You'll have to get past his bombshell secretary, over a silly spat or four, and solve Your Guy's aversion to living on a budget. You will have to decide where to hang your hats, or what to do when one of you gets a career opportunity across the country. Sometimes marriage will be work, other times it will feel like a slumber party for two. Most days it will feel like heaven. Every once in a blue moon you will want to run away from the house as fast as possible. Always, however, you will know that you're the best thing to ever happen to each other. Now that you finally found your partner in crime, you have so much to look forward to. This is only the beginning. And lucky you, you have the example of the Thoroughly Modern Married Girl to see you through.

TRADITIONAL OR CONTEMPORARY?

Thoroughly Modern Married Girls know matronly is *not* the meaning of matrimony. Instead they're breaking the old rules and making up new ones. Here's a look at how a Thoroughly Modern MG's wedded life differs from the Old-Fashioned Married Girl's:

Old-Fashioned Married Girl	Thoroughly Modern Married Girl
Depends on her husband's salary	Depends on her stockbroker
Drops her single girl friends as soon as she's hitched	Drops her circle of male admirers as soon as she's hitched
Believes a woman's place is in the home	Believes a woman's place is wherever she happens to be
Has a hot meal waiting for her man every night	Asks her guy what's for dinner
Only socializes in couples	Realizes life is not Noah's Ark
Says "I do" to her man and "I don't" to her career	Says "I do" to her man, her Muse, *and* her mentor
Makes babies on the honeymoon	Figures they'd better have plenty of practice first

CHAPTER ONE

The First Day of the Rest of Your Life Together

Mrs. Who? To Name Change or Not

One of your first big decisions as a dynamic duo is to decide what your new handle will be. Some of you Married Girls were ready to link your first names with his last the very second Your Guy first sent a sexy smile your way. For other MGs the decision is angst ridden and goes against everything you (and your shrink) have programmed your single selves to believe. Admittedly, sound dating mantras like "Don't lose yourself in the relationship" and "You shouldn't have to give up your identity to be with someone" loom large as you debate giving up the name you've known your whole life. Many MGs love the romance of becoming a unit and having a shared last name that they will pass on to their children. Others couldn't care less what anyone will think if they keep their monogram the way it was on their baby pillow.

Your Guy may or may not have very definite opinions about this, but this is one of the first big decisions you make together (you both have to live with your choice every day). So make sure you know his take. You can always remind him that legally he has the option to take *your* name. Whether you decide to keep the name your parents gave you or take on his, here's the skinny on what to expect:

TRADITIONAL

Mrs. Susie Marriedgirl

Taking on your husband's name is the biggest seller with new brides. Out of all your options it involves the least amount of speculation and questioning from pesky characters like your new mother-in-law.

PROS: This is an opportunity to align yourself with your man, the two of you against the world. It is especially useful if you have a notorious past, say, in the criminal underworld. You can erase it all with a new name (it's what cons on the run do, after all). And it is an especially tempting choice if you've been dying to get rid of an impossibly long or trickily spelled name.

CONS: You'll be faced with a few annoying transitional weeks, perhaps months, where you'll be constantly reminding people that your name isn't Susie Singlegirl anymore. You will be doing so much correcting you will feel like a third-grade teacher (or your mother). Old friends may not be supportive of your eliminating your Singlegirl roots. They might say, quite offhandedly, "You know, you'll always be Susie Singlegirl to me."

TIPS: This is a terrific opportunity to make over your office. Why not order new stationery, business cards, and an email address to assist in drilling your new surname into people's minds? There is something about seeing it in writing that makes things stick.

UNTRADITIONAL

Ms. Susie Singlegirl

Keeping your name is the way to go if you start to break out in hives, rashes, or cold sweats at the thought of losing the name you've had for the past twenty or thirty years. If you feel that your lovely name is inextricably linked to your identity, this is for you.

PROS: A good choice if you've established yourself publicly as a witty writer, sultry actor, or crime-fighting lawyer. And you don't have to go through the time-intensive process of changing your name on everything from your gym card to your Visa. A special plus if your husband's last name rhymes with your first name or is something less than desirable like Butt.

CONS: More traditional girls and your new mother-in-law will be openly disapproving. Be prepared for them to use guilt-inducing tactics like asking why you wouldn't want to take your husband's last name since it represents being committed to the relationship. You will have to make a very big point of introducing yourself as Susie Singlegirl lest people just assume you changed your name (like the emcee at the wedding probably did). This can be exasperating. Also, not a good option if you like using Your Guy's AmEx.

TIPS: Have a ready answer as to why you've decided not to change your name since you will constantly be explaining yourself. Something like "I don't want to change my name in case we get a divorce" will immediately stop anyone from bugging you about it.

HAVING IT BOTH WAYS

Ms. Susie Singlegirl for Work

Mrs. Susie Marriedgirl for Your Personal Life

Have the best of both worlds. Keep the name that has made you wildly successful in your career, but use your joint last name for social functions so single babes will know you two are together with a capital *T*.

PROS: You don't have to deal with the hassle of changing your name at work and having clients you've known forever say "Who?" when you call. You can go to parties and introduce yourself as Mrs. Marriedgirl to the delight of your mother-in-law. You can separate business from pleasure and have some anonymity in your personal life, key if you do something slightly naughty like write a sex column for *Playboy*.

CONS: You will feel like you are two people. Sybil but with only two personalities. There will be long awkward pauses before you introduce yourself, call anyone, make an appointment, or sign your name. You will constantly rack your brain when you see or talk to anyone and ponder, "Is this someone who knows me as Marriedgirl or Singlegirl?"

TIPS: Don't expect nine-to-five people to know what you call yourself from five to nine. Introducing yourself with just your first name saves a lot of migraines.

Mrs./Ms. Singlegirl-Marriedgirl

This seems like a good way to link the past with the future, but sometimes it seems a little forced. It's also, for whatever reason, not very glamorous.

PROS: People will still know it's you, as well as whom you've decided to commit to. It's a good way to keep everyone happy and mesh both your names into one.

CONS: Only works if both of you have shortish last names. Some last names simply don't go together but become tongue twisters when meshed. Do you really want to spell out Singlegirl-Marriedgirl when all you need is your dry-cleaning?

TIPS: For an easier time, have him hyphenate too.

CREATING A NEW NAME

Mr. and Mrs. Fantastic

You're a hip couple, so why not ignore convention and coin your own nifty handle? Try combining the beginning of one of your surnames with the end of the other. Or start fresh. Look in the phone book for a particular name that sounds like it's got "happy couple" written all over it and choose that.

PROS: You're on equal footing with each other since you're both tossing your former last names to the scrap heap. It's a chance to have the name you've always wanted (or at least a better one than you've got now). Your new handle may lead you in new and exciting directions, who knows? After all, would Veronica Lake have been a star if her name had stayed Constance Ockleman?

CONS: Your families will say things like "Our name isn't good enough for you?" Others, too, might consider it a little bizarre to suddenly adopt a new name. People might speculate the IRS is on your trail.

THE MG FILES:

Panic Attack at City Hall

It seemed innocent enough. Take a day off from work. Grab My Guy and head down to City Hall to get our marriage license and fill out some pesky name-change paperwork. No big deal. After seventeen years of debate, I had finally made a decision. At age ten, I told my mother that I would NEVER change my name (I also said I would always live at home). At age twenty-one, several college women's studies classes reinforced the ideal of not losing my surname to a patriarchal, chauvinistic ritual designed to obliterate the female's identity apart from her husband (even though I really, really wanted to join the patriarchal institution of wedlock). Most important, everyone called me Bliss.

Then, fabulous fate intervened and I got engaged to My Guy. I was past the feminist theory—working life had made me secure in my independent identity—but I didn't want to lose my nom de plume. Since My Guy is Mr. Mellow the idea that I might keep my name didn't faze him. "You're a writer, you've got to keep your by-

line," he said. My Guy was supportive, and très cool about whatever choice I made.

Age twenty-seven, my bridal shower. As soon as I looked at a monogrammed hand towel with my married initials on it, the Martha Stewart in me came out screaming. So cute! I loved the way it looked. I wanted to monogram everything. I wanted a welcome mat, stationery, and a mailbox with our new name on it. I wanted to be Mrs. Marriedgirl and I couldn't wait to have little babes and send out Marriedgirl family holiday cards.

I was conflicted. What's a Thoroughly Modern Almost Married Girl to do?

By the time I got up to the counter at City Hall I was ready with my name-change form filled out as Sara Bliss Marriedgirl. My Guy loved our decision: use his last name socially and as a family, and use Bliss for churning out the great American novel. "I need to be anonymous when you're famous," he said, grinning.

Government Red Tape Lady quickly put a stop to our plans. "You can hyphenate. You can't make your maiden name your middle name unless you ask permission of the court," she pronounced. "What's it going to be?" In the past weeks, I had endured not fitting into my wedding dress because I had gained weight, bridesmaids' skirts that arrived see-through, and now this. Red Tape Lady watched me panic.

I hesitated. I hemmed and hawed. I stared blankly at the paper before me. My Guy awaited my decision. Red Tape Lady was not so patient. She suggested we step aside and loudly announced that we were wasting both her time and the time of other "ready and organized" brides.

We were banished to the corner of the room to figure things out. Other brides sent concerned glances our way. My Guy found the whole thing very amusing. He let me know that things could be worse, I could be embarking on life with Menacing Tattoo Muscle Guy across the room.

End result? Red Tape Lady let us come back to the counter. I didn't let a little hyphen become a big problem. Now I'm three people. Hyphengirl for legal documents. Marriedgirl for family life. Bliss for my pen name. But my friends and My Guy still call me Bliss.

Leaving the Spotlight

When you return ecstatic from your honeymoon, don't make the mistake of thinking that the world still revolves around the two of you and your great love for each other. It's easy to think that all time has stopped. You haven't seen Peter Jennings for weeks, didn't call a soul, and spent most of your time lounging on the beach/skiing down the slopes/trekking the third world/checking in to country inns. However, the reality is that everyone at home has moved on.

When you walk into a party after you're married expect a quick congratulations and a "Your wedding was so beautiful." Don't expect the same obsession with you and your wedding as when you got engaged. After Your Guy popped the question didn't you feel like a movie starlet on a publicity tour? Friends and family wanted to hear all the details: Did he get down on bended knee? Were you surprised? Emerald or princess cut? Carats? Town or country nuptials?

Vera? What time of day? Hair up or down? What shade of pink exactly? Chocolate or lemon icing? And on and on and on. This fascination with you ends after the wedding and poof! You're again just like everyone else.

After spending months listening to you talk in painstaking detail about your every fight with the caterer, your friends may be a little bored with you two. Now the latest obsession is over the new fall lineup: your friend Lucinda who's finally pregnant (with twins!) or your cousin Isabella's second wedding to an English lord. You and Your Guy are just reruns. Your buddies will want to hear from you when you return from Bora Bora so they can tell you, yes, how marvelous your wedding was and how beautiful you looked, but mainly that they started dating Your Guy's cute cousin. Then you should (quickly) mention how romantic your honeymoon was, but that's it. You may have a few saintly friends who will wade through hundreds of wedding photos (although probably just to see pictures of them dancing with Your Guy's cute cousin). Only your parents will be really eager to see the pics, since it's likely they contributed some chunk of cash to the event, and they want proof of where it all went.

The MG Blues

Lots of Married Girls get a little bummed out when they realize they will never again be a bride. No more moonlit proposals. No more being the star. No more showers (you'll have to get pregnant for another one of those). No more parties in your honor. The Post-

Wedding Blues is a common, but little-discussed phenomenon. Symptoms include secretly continuing to buy *Martha Stewart Weddings*, trying to schedule lunch with your wedding planner because you miss seeing her, and going to bridal fairs just to know what's going on in the market. Don't think that Your Guy is going to feel the same post-wedding doldrums. He is probably thrilled that all the wedding nonsense is over. After all, he just wanted you to say "I do."

Get over the Post-Wedding Blues by living vicariously through someone else's wedding. Engaged girls are always happy for another opinion and you're now a pro. Let them have a moment to shine while you take a back seat as simply a fountain of good info. Give them your wedding sources, the scoop on handling pre-wedding jitters, and the pros and cons of a receiving line. If you're still pining for wedding festivities, throw a newly engaged couple a rockin' engagement party. Just don't expect any more showering *you* with gifts, compliments, rose petals, and applause (although you could ask Your Guy to keep this up indefinitely).

Don't Bother Us, We're Busy Living Happily Ever After

Now that you're embarking on life as a Thoroughly Modern Married Couple, it is time to envision how you want your happily-ever-after to be. From free time to the daily grind, from the practical to the preposterous, give some thought to imagining an anti-cookie-cutter life that suits you both. Did you always dream of touring through

Italy by bicycle or spending a year somewhere you don't speak the language? Does Your Guy want to keep up with his weekly surfing jaunts and open a little surf shack someday? Write yourselves a "life will," a list of all the things you two *will* do in your life together. No need to figure out exactly *how* you're going to realize all your wild ideas, just jot it all down. Your list should answer the question "If we could do absolutely anything at all, what would it be?"

Your life will is a sassy life map that ensures that you are the designers of your own unique universe. Be sure to cover daily issues (switch to all organic) as well as job dreams (ditch the nine to five gigs and write novels), hopes for kids (at least four and they'll be trilingual), ideas for travel (take a year to "study abroad"), and house hopes (design and build your own). You guys can update it every year without deleting any of the ideas you initially conjured up. If you follow your plan more or less, on your fiftieth wedding anniversary you won't look back wistfully, realizing that you haven't done anything except head for the office. Instead, when you're old (and still blond) you might see that you've checked off a hefty percentage of your list. You're a dynamic duo now, so why not shoot for the stars?

THOROUGHLY MODERN MARRIED COUPLES
IN THE SPOTLIGHT

A Thoroughly Modern Couple knows that there's plenty of room for two stars to shine in a marriage. They write their own rules for a successful partnership, support each other's crazy dreams, and at the end of the day know there is nothing better than having someone who loves you even when the chips (or your box office stats) are down. As for Loni, Pamela, Carmen, and Ivana—sorry girls. You signed on for alpha males at their worst, and we can only wish you luck the next time around.

Thoroughly Modern Marriages

Sarah Jessica Parker and Matthew Broderick

Tracy Pollan and Michael J. Fox

Jennifer Aniston and Brad Pitt

Kelly Ripa and Mark Consuelos

Hilary Swank and Chad Lowe

Uma Thurman and Ethan Hawke

Jada Pinkett Smith and Will Smith

Téa Leoni and David Duchovny

Heather Locklear and Ritchie Sambora

Sofia Coppola and Spike Jonze

Thorougly Modern Mentors

Joanne Woodward and Paul Newman

Anne Bancroft and Mel Brooks

Rita Wilson and Tom Hanks

Trudie Styler and Sting

Thoroughly Surprising Divorces

Lucille Ball and Desi Arnaz

Nicole Kidman and Tom Cruise

Meg Ryan and Dennis Quaid

Patricia Arquette and Nicolas Cage

Princess Diana and Prince Charles

Cindy Crawford and Richard Gere

Thoroughly Messy Marriages

Loni Anderson and Burt Reynolds

Pamela Anderson and Tommy Lee

Carmen Electra and Dennis Rodman

Ivana and Donald Trump

CHAPTER TWO

Becoming a Domestic Goddess

Buying Your Love Nest

When you were single, you thought nothing of paying two-thirds of your monthly income to live in a so-so apartment with three other girls and one pretty gross bathroom. Your humungous rent was just a given, like coffee in the morning, but it put you in the middle of your town's action and that's the only place you wanted to be. Now suddenly you're a Married Girl and there are two salaries and two life savings to squander on living arrangements and it starts to go to your head. You don't want to rent anymore. You want to buy. You want to own something substantial (besides you engagement ring). You want a whole *room* to store your wedding china, not a box tucked under the bed in your teensy apartment. So, now you're in the market for a love shack. You're going to single-handedly stimulate the lagging economy—you're doing your patriotic duty by buying, after all. The two of you will be *homeowners* (a condo is still a home, right?).

You two may enter the real estate process assuming that finding a little love nest is simply a matter of spotting a dream pad, placing an offer, and picking out curtains. Ha! Instead, searching for a place will involve chronic anxiety about late payments from 1998 that are ruining your credit, worry that you will never find a place you remotely like, and stress that if you actually do buy something, it will turn out to have termites or be next door to an underground brothel.

House hunting, like husband hunting, can be an obsession that leads straight to your therapist's couch. "But that house was supposed to be ours!" you wail to your beyond-bored doctor, your equally frustrated husband, or anyone on the bus who will listen to your tales from the real estate side. Trying to afford and locate the right house will not only feel like a second job but it will take over your real job, your social life, and all your free time. A little like wedding planning, actually. Real estate searches begin at the crack of dawn, when, still essentially asleep, Your Guy goes online scouring the local paper's real estate listings in order to beat everyone else to the latest pads on the market. When he spots something that sounds great, "hardwood floors, sunny, and spacious," he puts you to work leaving long rambling messages for the broker at his office, while looking up his home number in the phone book. When you do get to the business of placing an offer, you find yourself using never-fail flirtation techniques you read about in *Cosmo* on the homeowner (If the owner is a woman, this task falls on Your Guy). That way if someone places the same bid they'll remember you two sexy things and possibly pick you over someone who was, let's say, less appealing.

In your crazed real estate of mind, you've forgotten about your true friends and instead become best buds with the local star broker, who's twenty years older and notoriously annoying. You bake her triple layer cakes from scratch, invite her to your shindigs, and even listen to her complain ad nauseam about her hellish husband. All this so she'll call you first when an unbelievable place comes up. You and Your Guy have both even mastered the art of faking out your competition at an open house. "Oh honey, this looks like it would need at *least* $200,000 in renovations to make it barely livable!" you gasp in horror before shouting, "Look at those roaches!" Of course, Your Guy knows this is code for "Let's make an offer, stat!"

Sticker Shock

The Olympic sport of real estate buying in popular Thoroughly Modern MG cities like Manhattan and San Francisco can be especially cutthroat. First off, you have to deal with being thoroughly discouraged, depressed, and despondent when you see what you can actually afford. Even if you have spotless credit, cash stashed away, and are willing to commit your lifetime earnings in advance, it's never enough. There is always an apartment $100,000 more than your budget, that's so much better than the sad, dark, cramped place in your price range. It's enough to make a decidedly East Coast couple move out to the Dakotas, where sixty acres costs less than a thousand square feet in Beantown. The few (very few) decently priced places that don't have brown tiles, closets that could only hold a toothbrush, and wall-to-wall green shag carpet assume mythological status. And be prepared to find that all the other MGs want the same type of pad you want: pre-war in Manhattan, Left Bank walk-up in Paris, and Art Deco in Miami. Beware of Impossibly Smug Married Girls trying to ply you with Cosmopolitans to find out where you're looking. As soon as you mention the crown moldings, working fireplace, and a sub zero, Impossibly Smug will turn on her stilettos and be out the door hunting down the broker. A savvy MG knows that she only talks real estate with her hubby and her agent until the deal is closed.

Deciding Where to Hang Your Hats: City MGs vs. Country MGs

Is your fantasy life played out in the concrete jungle or in the roaring jungle? Do you see yourself in Paris, chic and skinny, armed with sunglasses and a baguette, smooching Your Guy on the banks of the Seine? Or would you prefer to live in Virginia horse country looking glam in jodhpurs enjoying wine and brie picnics with Your Guy? Are you a city or a country MG? Whether you choose the wilderness or the wild city, the day-to-day grind will be totally different. From how you spend your free time to the pros and cons of each choice, here's the real deal on what a Married Girl can expect from each vantage point:

CITY MARRIED GIRL will tell you how hip and happening urban life is. Living in a sixth-floor walk-up with mice? No problem, they're never in the apartment anyway. Paying big bucks for small space? They insist that the benefits of having an amazing symphony, the nation's best spa, and the hottest restaurants only a few blocks away are worth every c-note. The city MG loves being able to get everywhere in ten minutes and never having to worry about parking. Everything at her fingertips makes her happily spoiled, and spoiled is the way she likes it. When she leaves the city she mourns the loss of four-star French bistros that are open till 4 A.M., indie movie theaters that serve chai, and Barnes & Noble's same-day delivery. She simply calls her city "The City," every place else is "The Country." She loves to visit The Country but couldn't possibly live there. The wilderness is bearable to the city MG only if there is a romantic inn

involved. She fears strip malls, malls in general, cookie-cutter con-
dos, and life behind the wheel of a minivan. Besides, how could she
wear her strappy silk stiletto Manolos in the grass?

COUNTRY MARRIED GIRL raves about how stress-free, green, and
spacious rural living is. Since she gets more for her $$ in the burbs,
she has more $$ than strapped-for-cash city MGs. She uses the extra bucks to throw chic garden parties lit by Moroccan lanterns, hire
a trendy designer to transform her pad, and jet off to the latest *Condé
Nast Traveler* hotspot for some playtime with her hubby. The less
hectic, less crazy vibe of country life appeals to her. Country MG
spends her time painting scenic vistas, hosting croquet matches, and
scaling peaks and valleys to camp out with her country man. She
doesn't like city crowds, or subway stations that smell like pee.
Country MG knows what to do if she encounters a grizzly, but she's
not so sure how to handle a mugger, so she always goes to the urban
jungle with Mace tucked into her Coach bag. Besides, when she's in
the city she has to wear heels when she would much rather be running barefoot in the grass.

When the City Mouse Marries the Country Mouse (a Fable)

Sometimes the city mouse and country mouse can't help but fall in
love. For most of their mousy lives they just assumed they would end
up with the mouse next door. But love caught them by surprise. The
native New Yorker mouse is so enamored with the Montana-born-

and-bred country mouse that she wants to learn what really makes him tick. She finds herself careening at terrifying speeds and night-mare-inducing heights in a hang glider strapped to her guy. She learns how to ride horses bareback without breaking a rib, fly-fish in river rapids without breaking a nail, and how to survive in the wilder-ness without dying (a skill she hopes she will never have to test). When she arrives donning Jimmy Choo boots to scale a peak, she learns spike heels are not considered appropriate hiking attire.

The country mouse becomes even more wildly in love when he sees that she's not just a city slicker. She can chat with the cowboys, shoot skeet like a pro, and two-step with the best of them. Besides, it's hard not to adore city mouse when she's slipping on rocks, falling down ski slopes, and running after a horse she has just fallen off of, all in the name of love.

The country mouse learns to love the finer points of the city. He learns that he looks good in a suit, that shopping is a form of exercise, and that roaming around the Met is as exhausting as climbing a mountain. She loves that he's not just a country bumpkin. He's ready to try any new trend she sends his way whether it's poetry slams, oxy-gen bars, or crystal healing. Plus he's got all her city micette pals swooning from his laid-back country charm.

So—where to live? Country mouse has visions of barbecues on the deck after work, mountain biking on weekends, and children—someday—running through sprinklers on the front lawn. City mouse envisions grabbing a drink at the corner bistro after work, ex-ploring art galleries on the weekends, and children—someday—swimming at the rooftop pool. What to do?

City mouse probably wouldn't be happy in a cabin with moose out back in Montana. Country mouse might not enjoy living in Trump Tower with Yorkshire terriers on the terrace. For city mouse and country mouse to coexist in bliss, they need to find some middle ground. A little city living needs to be brought to the country and vice versa. Eva Gabor, an MG role model for sure, was able to bring a little of "Pahhhhhk Avenue, dahling," to Green Acres, donning fur-trimmed mules, diamonds, and feather boas to milk the cows.

If country mouse has to live in the urban jungle, the pair must find a place with a view of the park, or river, or, preferably, it's own little garden. Ideally, there's room to plunk down a Weber grill because even if he didn't shoot it himself, there's nothing like grilled venison. City living must seem as unclaustrophobic as possible. Even in the ultimate urban jungle, New York City, there are opportunities for country mouse to express his sporty self. He can kayak on the Hudson, horseback ride in Central Park, and scale the climbing wall at the Equinox. Alternate-side parking may be hell, but a car is a must for weekend escapes to trout fish, snowshoe, or build cabins in the woods with his bare hands (evenings are spent by the fire at a B&B of city mouse's own choosing). If city mouse hauls it out to the country to live, she should be only a quick train or plane ride from blessed concrete pavements and the magical beauty department at Bergdorf's. Minimum, she's got to have her outlets. When she's away from the city, the City MG is happy to discover that she can read the *New York Post*'s gossip column, PageSix online, and that H&H Bagels will ship overnight. But most important, city mouse and country mouse know that life in their natural habitats would be nothing without their true love.

And city mouse and country mouse live mousily ever after.

Designing Couples: Creating a Pad That Suits Both Your Styles

Whether your first place is a deluxe apartment in the sky or you're living on love in a little fixer-upper off the highway, now you've got to paint it, fix it, and fill it up with stuff. Jump into domestic life with the digits of a savvy real estate agent, some tough movers, and great gourmet takeout. Inspire yourself by watching the Style channel for fashionista 411 and *Trading Spaces* for unfashionable but nevertheless clever transformations. And don't forget to steal glamorous ideas from the pages of *Elle Decor*, and borrow a few do-it-yourself tips (not stock tips) from the Diva of Domesticity's *Martha Stewart Living*.

Once you're ready to become a domestic goddess you've got to factor in Your Guy's taste and try to mesh it with your own. Designing a place that suits both your styles makes finding love look easy. He may like red, you might prefer blue. You might vibe with stripes and he might dig chintz. Just because you two see eye to eye, doesn't mean your taste does. Depending on Your Guy's design IQ, here's what to expect when you dive into the world of fabric swatches and paint chips:

YOUR GUY'S GOT NO STYLE

You lovebirds may adore a million of the same things—that little gem of a Left Bank hotel you stayed in on your honeymoon in Paris, yellow labs, and high-speed rollercoasters—but your style sense may be ready for a divorce. Your sans-style guy thinks a rickety futon or a loft with a ladder is the way to sleep. He may actually believe living with mustard-colored bathroom tiles, Romanesque columns, and polyester yellow-and-black sheets left behind by the previous occupants is perfectly OK. You will have frequent discussions that involve him uttering "But we have a (insert furniture type here) that is perfectly fine, why do we need to spend money on a new (insert furniture type here)?" This is hard to argue with. Practicality vs. style is a tough battle. It is also particularly frightening for the Thoroughly Modern MG, who spent years honing her style and isn't about to let things slide now. Your job is to try to show him the design light and save his nonstylish soul. Take him shopping for the whole day (just make sure he doesn't look at the prices). Have him recline on a luxury mattress (try the Ritz hotels' exclusive Sealy mattress), examine gorgeous antiques at auction (Christie's has great catalogs), or see the potential in vintage treasures at the flea market (buy Rachel Ashwell's *Shabby Chic* before you go). After a whole day of shopping there will be one of two outcomes:

A) He is incredibly bored and exhausted and never wants to look at furniture and fabrics again. Success! You will be in charge from here on out.

B) Once he discovers sleeping on high-thread-count sheets, and the benefits of having enough chairs to host a dinner party, he won't want to go back to bachelor pad design. He may even take the credit when friends come over and admire your swanky pad.

YOUR GUY'S GOT NO STYLE BUT THINKS HE DOES

This is the worst-case scenario. He hasn't got a clue but he thinks he is Mario Buatta. He wants to decorate your house with duck decoys, Bob Marley posters, or reproduction gothic-style chairs that he thinks are priceless antiques. Your Guy has got a bad case of bad style. Your Guy wants to be involved in all design decisions, in fact, he wants to inflict his own bad taste on you. He may even point out pieces of *your* furniture that he wants to get rid of. Many Married Girls have found the solution is hiring a decorator. Of course, interview the designers first to ensure that they see eye to eye with your style, and not his, otherwise this plan could backfire. A savvy designer will listen to how you each envision your place (you think midcentury modern, he thinks hunting lodge style) and come up with a solution that you both love (duck-themed powder room with Eames staples in the living room). The decorator can prevent a myriad of potential arguments, since you never have to tell Your Guy he doesn't get it. That's your decorator's job. You can just say, "I can't believe our designer didn't want to use your stuffed wall-mounted moose head! What a pity!"

YOUR GUY'S GOT STYLE

Some of you Married Girls have the design stars on your side. Your Guy's mother is a decorator, his uncle owns a French antique store, or Your Guy is a hip furniture designer. In this case, you have it made. Bolts of extra fabric, sample furniture, and lovely antiques are constantly handed to you. Your Guy has great taste and knows the difference between a Bergère and a burger, as well as Billy Baldwin the famous decorator and Billy the Baldwin brother. The only downside is that if he's in the business and you're not, your taste may have to take a back seat to his or his family's professional opinion. If you have been given a houseful of his family heirlooms but you prefer modern, you can't haul everything to Sotheby's. You can, however, spice things up by upholstering the Louis XVI side chair in a graphic modern pattern or a saucy leopard print.

MG

Design Bibles

While the MG has an innate sense of style, she always looks to the masters for inspiration. Whether she relies on David Hicks' timeless style or Carolyne Roehm's society style, the MG has both old and new design bibles to see her through. Whether you want some hands-on decorating advice from Mark Hampton or to try some new looks from an exotic locale, here are a few essentials to pile on your coffee table:

***Billy Baldwin Decorates,* Billy Baldwin**

Visual inspiration on the do's of design.

***Bright Young Things,* Brooke De Ocampo**

Chic, smug, married Brooke explores the homes of her style maven friends in New York and London.

***Color,* Donald Kaufman and Taffy Dahl**

Color maestro Kaufman's luscious palettes are eye candy for design lovers.

***David Hicks Living With Design,* David Hicks**

Hicks' rooms transcend trends to achieve timeless elegance.

***Designing Women,* Margaret Russell**

A look into the homes and style secrets of today's top female designers.

***Mark Hampton On Decorating,* Mark Hampton**

A design master's wisdom.

***Paris Interiors; Indian Interiors;* and *Moroccan Interiors,* published by Taschen**

For adding some exotic flair to your pad.

***Seasonal Notebooks,* Carolyne Roehm**

Blooms, recipes, and lifestyle tips for every season.

Getting Rid of His La-Z-Boy
Without Starting a Riot

When you were dating you didn't mind it. Well, you thought it was atrocious but you didn't have to live with it. You assumed that the ugly, plaid, purple and black and beige recliner was something he owned because he didn't have the time or the inclination to shop for *real* furniture. You *never* imagined that he would pack it in the moving van, haul it to your new place, and place it smack in front of the tube. "But I love this chair!" he will exclaim to poor horrified you. He will point out the speakers in the headrest, the heated seat, and the double beer can holder. Even if Your Guy dresses impeccably and always picks out the most beautiful gifts, many a Married Guy's style sense goes out the window when it comes to furniture. The recliner may have a foul odor, inexplicable stains, and tears in the upholstery and he will still fight to keep it. You have to realize that it's not about the chair at all. It's about clinging to his single self. His self that didn't have to answer to anyone, ate burgers for breakfast, and could own the damn ugliest chair in the world if he wanted to. No one was there to stop him.

Now *you* have to stop him. Your ideal decorating scheme is a spirited mix. You may have a flair for the exotic, lavishing your pad with sumptuous Indian fabrics, Turkish-tile-topped tables, and batik pillows. You might be more of a classic girl, loving toile textiles, anything from the Paris flea markets, and English antiques inherited from your Park Avenue grandmother. Perhaps you're a contemporary diva collecting a sleek ceramics, groovy retro print rugs, and some colorful Italian modern furniture. Whatever your style, you never factored in a La-Z-Boy in the living room. Now, how to get rid of that eyesore he adores, seemingly more than you?

You have a few options here. If you have a basement, give that to him. Tell him he can create his own universe down there. He can design it with animal heads, dartboards, jukeboxes, leather furniture, and neon Budweiser signs as long as you get to be in charge of everything else. Don't you dare go down there, it will be too scary for words. It will remind you of a frat house. Warning: other Married Guys will congregate there as they try to escape from uncomfortable (but great looking!) MG furniture.

One smart MG surveyed her husband's frightening inflatable furniture, baseball hat collection, and other relics from bachelorhood and simply brought them downstairs to the storage room one by one. She knew that if he noticed anything missing she could always retrieve the object and bring it upstairs. He never noticed.

The best option, however, is not to let an undesirable object out of the moving van. Simply give the offending item away to the moving men (although you may have to pay them extra to get rid of it, it's worth every penny). Just tell Your Guy that it never arrived. "Terrible news! It was lost or irreparably damaged! Freak storm blew it away! A gang of bank robbers shot holes in it! Someone just offered me $300 for it!" Show him the cash.

Why Don't You Cook? No Thanks, Honey, Why Don't You? Negotiating Household Tasks

When you're dating, it's all about the love, it's never about the dishes. When you're married you will have evenings that revolve entirely around your dishes: why they are sitting in the sink, who should be responsible for washing them, and debating why you own a dishwasher if you still have to clean the plates beforehand. It's all very unsexy. The amount of discussion that goes on about household tasks is a shock to the MG. When you were single, you didn't talk with your beau about the merits of Windex, you simply put things away (or at least under the bed), and pulled out the Dustbuster every once in a while. When you two spent an evening together you talked about the faults in the president's environmental policy, why you both love Robert Altman films, and how fantastic being married would be. Now, at some point on a given evening, debate time that was once reserved for more intellectually challenging topics goes to discussing whose turn it is to clean up.

The constant discussions about mundane household issues are a good example of realities your MG friends never discussed with you when you didn't have a ring on your finger. When you asked about married life they would giggle, blush, and say it was wonderful and that they highly recommended it. They never talked about the dishes. When you now ask why they never brought this up, they say that they didn't want to scare you. It's a little like pregnancy, there are some things you don't want to know about until there's no turning back.

HINDSIGHT IS 20/20

In an ideal marriage you both have some domestic skills, and hopefully they mesh. When you cook, he cleans (and cooking includes dialing up for Pad Thai). If you do the laundry, he puts it away. If he polishes the silver, you throw a dinner party. Some Married Guys are fabulous around the house. If only you had known to look for this when you were single. Neat, Organized, and Handy with a Mop should have been on your list, right alongside (if not above) Funny Handsome, and Athletic. If you both like to do (or are able to do) different chores, things will get accomplished without a tantrum that involves somebody throwing the dishes across the room and telling the other person to clean up.

DIAL-A-WIFE

As an MG you don't mind cleaning now and then (with the emphasis on "then" and not "now"), but you want him to know that it's your *choice* to tidy up. Even if you are obsessively neat, you don't *have* to be scrubbing the toilet. You're not a fifties housewife. Your Guy has the same obligation to scrub the toilet as you do. You believe in equality in the marriage. You two use words like "team," "partner," "soulmate." So when he expects you to fry up the bacon *and* clean up the pan, you draw the line. You went into marriage with the idea that everything should be fifty-fifty. Now that you're hitched you realize that fifty-fifty is a bit of a myth. There is always someone who gets stuck with 70 percent. Hopefully that someone is not you.

The answer, the MG learns, is to make the pie smaller—fewer tasks, less to divide. Not all MGs are handy with a broom. Many are just as unschooled in the domestic arts as their men. You may be a fantastic decorator, ready with a staple gun for quick upholstery jobs, savvy about building shelves, and a pro with a floor sander. You may even be a fab stylist. You can arrange flowers like a florist, expertly frame and arrange pics along a wall, or reorganize a bookshelf to display the classics rather than your Danielle Steels. But your version of whipping up dinner may involve whipping out the menus and dialing for takeout. Your method of hosting Thanksgiving may be to call your wedding caterer (she does turkeys, too). Laundry may involve sorting out the whites and darks and dropping them off at the local Laundromat. Cleaning up to you sometimes means washing your hands of having to actually clean. Life is short, and the MG and Her Guy know that shortcuts are indispensable paths to harmonious living.

THE GLAM HOUSEWIFE

If you have to clean even half the house, you might as well look good doing it. Treat yourself to a red organza ruffled apron and a matching feather duster. There are loads of ridiculous high-end cleaning products designed to make cleaning feel chic. Lavender-scented water for ironing, organic glass cleaner, linen dish towels, and sunflower-shaped sink stoppers—who cares if it's clean when it looks and smells this good?

THE MG FILES:

The Odd Couple

OK, I admit it. I'm not the neatest person in the world. When I was in college my friends would marvel at how I could emerge looking so pulled-together from my tornado of a room. The price of looking chic in the outside world was tissues on the floor, crumbled-up papers everywhere but the wastebasket, a chronically unmade bed, and a copy of Vogue smearing newsprint under the covers. I was always late because something was invariably lost. I could never locate my keys, wallet, or the ten-page paper I had just written. I always thought I had better things to be doing with my time than cleaning (like trying on lipstick colors, trying to write like Cynthia Heimel, and flirting with the cute guy in Spanish class). I did, however, clean whenever I had a date coming to pick me up or someone I didn't know well stopping by. While I didn't mind my sloppiness, I didn't want other people to be horrified by it.

When My Guy arrived on the scene, I found out he was disgustingly neat—clean, even. He devised closet-organization systems, never lost his car in the parking lot, and actually owned mops, vacuums, and a bucket of cleaning fluids (which he used himself!). Since we were friends long before we dated, My Guy knew about my messy tendencies. But still, even he had limits. There was nothing worse than seeing My Guy's shocked face when he opened my fridge to discover dirty dishes. I thought (at the time) that this was a very clever alternative to leaving dirty pots in the sink waiting for *bugs. But after seeing his expression, I decided then and there that I didn't want to be Oscar to his Felix. Also, I didn't want my messy ways to be the deal breaker in our otherwise fabulous relationship. I took on some magazine assignments on clutter control and read up on feng shui (clutter blocks creative and sexual energy, according to the masters). I made an effort to be neater (fabric-covered boxes for storage are a great trick). But the best thing I did was to become very good friends with the very discreet dial-a-housekeeper. A messy Married Girl's shameless addiction.*

Designing the Argument-Free House

You'll realize when you're living married that there are dependable household triggers for major spats. If you can afford to make a few changes, your marriage will thank you.

SEPARATE BATHROOMS

Ask any woman married more than ten years the secret to her successful union, and she'll tell you that she owes it all to separate bathrooms. When you share a bathroom with Your Guy, you have to duke it out for the shower, same goes for the sink, and as for time in front of the mirror, forget it. There are also things about your husband that you don't need to know. His bathroom adventures should be his own private matter and if he has his own toilet in another part of the house, they can remain private.

MAJOR APPLIANCES

Dishwashers, washers, and dryers go a long way toward creating household harmony. Dishes won't get piled in the sink waiting to get washed. Laundry can get cleaned immediately rather than waiting three days for the Laundromat to get to it. Of course you both have to learn how to use these appliances, but after handwashing for years and lugging twenty-pound sacks to the corner, rinsing, loading, and unloading won't seem like a big deal.

QUEEN-SIZED BEDS

If you get a full-sized bed, you're going to be battling it out for space every night. Not much better with a king. Sure you'll have more room, but you'll have so much space you won't feel like you're in the same bed. You might even feel like you're in bed alone—no fun. Queen-sized beds are perfect. Close enough so there will be lots of snuggling but big enough that you have space to stretch out.

CHAPTER THREE

Family Matters

Family Ties: Tying the Knot with Your Guy and His Family

When you marry into his family and he marries into yours, you're no longer in the deliciously private world of dating. Indeed, your married world is unexpectedly crowded. His competitive sister, playboy father, wonderful mother, smug stepbrother and countless extras all come with Your Guy. The truth is, for better or worse, you don't just marry Your Guy, you marry his entire family. Sorry, honey, but it's a package deal.

It was so much easier when his family was merely the source of amusing and heart-wrenching anecdotes shared over dinner. But after he brought you home to meet his folks, you suddenly had a live cast of characters to contend with. Since you loved Your Guy and he loved them, not to mention valued their input, you did your best to look and act the part of future wife. You dressed to impress the family, replacing your usual super-low-slung jeans and perilously high heels in favor of the more parent-friendly Jackie O pearls and a shift dress. You tried your hardest to charm them by being breezy and entertaining, while they interviewed you as a potential candidate to award their cherished last name. The more serious you were with Your Guy, the more varsity the interview. His mother even concocted sneaky tests of your capability for the starring role as wife and the supporting role as daughter-in-law. The trickiest exam was to unexpectedly place her four-month-old granddaughter in your arms. If the baby wailed, this was minus two points for you. If the little babe cooed and gurgled, score ten points. The interrogation didn't end there; throughout the evening his parents played a game of two thousand questions. If you had been married before or ever had a job as a "dancer" your approval rating plummeted. Seemingly innocent questions like where you went to college were a crafty way for Your Guy's mom to figure out who she might know to get the inside scoop on you. As tough as they were, you were more eager to please. Even before you left, you were composing a thoughtful and gracious thank-you note in your head. Afterward, you desperately hoped at least one terribly insightful relative would pull Your Guy aside and gush, "She's incredible, don't you dare let her get away!"

After you passed the pop wife quiz and got engaged, the toasts were lavish and gushing. You thought your relationship with his clan would go on being blissful forever. You imagined taking long Saturday afternoon walks with your in-laws sharing insights into life, love, matrimony, and Your Guy. But instead, when you moved up to fiancée, the wedding spotlight hit the good, bad, and ugly sides of your future in-laws. His mother, who previously had complimented you on your "snappy outfits" suddenly blurted out that she thought your strapless wedding dress was "a bit much." His sister, who had formerly bonded with you over sample sales, complained that the bridesmaid's dress you picked out made her look hippy. Welcome to the family.

The Post-Wedding Rebound

Once you're married, you'll realize there's been a sneaky shift in power, and suddenly you hold all the cards. You and Your Guy are family now, and no matter how your in-laws feel, they still have to live with it. That kissing up and eagerness to please can rebound on you, and you may start to resent the very people whose good opinion you desperately sought. Advice from one MG to another? Get over it. It's natural to feel like you've run a gauntlet of irrelevant opinions to end up on this side of the married divide. But you're an MG now and you should still be gracious and generous even though you don't have to.

Everybody's a Critic: Dealing with Opinions Other Than Your Own

Now that you're family, no one feels the need to hold back anymore (sadly). His mother now critiques your miniskirt as being "too mini" and your job as "inappropriate for a married woman." Of course, your own family is also in on the action and predictably your mother has the opposite viewpoint as his. From your job to your cooking, to your plans for kids, everyone wants to chime in with their wisdom whether it's gleaned from Dr. Phil or their numerous marriages.

Many MGs and their men who previously only discussed superficialities with their in-laws are taken aback by their new families' expectations. Your in-laws may start conversations with "Well, in our family we do things this way . . ." or your family may use the more subtle but equally daunting "Now that you're married, you'll want to . . ." The fact that you're a successful executive (why, you just closed a million-dollar deal last week) and that you've managed to make wise choices (you're marrying Your Guy, after all) seems completely lost on everyone. While no one is harassing Your Guy about quitting his job after a baby is born, he may get pressure from your family to live up to financial expectations. You two can compare notes on which is worse, the baby speech or the money speech.

The way to handle this barrage of unsolicited advice into the most personal aspects of your lives is to always present a united front with Your Guy. When your father insists you live next door in a house he'll pay for, but you two would prefer your own little shack with no strings attached, you both want to say "Thanks, but no" with equal gusto. If Your Guy is on a different page about what to do, that's fine, but work it out at home. A little privacy goes a long way when it comes to relatives. Who wants not only their hubby disagreeing with them, but their whole family as well? Not you. When dealing with your families you both have to remember that you want to take their thoughts into consideration (they've guided you this far) but ultimately your decisions together are the most significant. You're grown-ups now, the wedding certificate made it official.

Loving His Mother Without Losing Your Mind

Even if she's a marvelous mother-in-law and the ultimate role model for an MG, it's a tricky relationship. She's not your mother, but she'll often act like she is and expect you to adhere to the gospel according to Her. It's a challenge for her to accept that she's no longer in charge and you guys aren't still "kids" (she may still refer to you as such). Ultimately, you must, in no uncertain terms, no matter what, get along with her, regardless of how high-maintenance or demanding she may be. Otherwise you risk putting Your Guy in the middle of two hotheaded women. Testing out his love for you by shouting "It's my way or her way!" is enough to make even the most stoic of husbands weep. Your Guy should never be expected to choose sides. What if he doesn't choose yours?

Part of loving Your Guy means loving his mother too. No matter how you feel about your mother-in-law, remember, without her there would be no him. You may believe it's a divine miracle that he turned out so great, but give her the credit. The fact that he stands up when you enter the room, knows how to vacuum, and gets you to smile even when you're sobbing, is due to her fine training. So treat the woman to a massage every now and then, she worked hard and you're reaping the benefits.

When confronted with a devastatingly difficult Mommie Dearest the MG tries her darndest. The first step is understanding why she's being a huge pain. Most likely it's a terrible fear that by her baby boy marrying little ol' you, he's going to abandon little ol' her. If Your Guy was an especially attentive son, the kind that drove her to her Tuesday bridge game without fault or fixed the roof, cleaned the gutters, and painted the house by hand, she's worried that it all will stop now that you're on the scene. Settle her fears. Show her you're not the enemy and that Your Guy isn't going to disappear into a cloud of wedding smoke. You can even reinforce that tired wedding cliché, and tell her she's not losing a son but gaining a daughter. If you live nearby, show her two is better than one by being just as fabulous as her son. Drive her to her Tuesday bridge game yourself, and pick up some flowers and a latte for her on your way. When Your Guy goes over to paint the house, throw on your overalls and get out your paintbrush.

Bond with her if at all possible. You never know, if you and Your Guy are ever on the rocks he may turn to her for advice, and you don't want her encouraging him to leave you behind! She did raise your husband so she was dealing with his tricks long before you came along. If you become her friend, she may have some tips for you. Whatever you do, avoid the urge to tell her you'll take it from here.

Best Friend? Nemesis? Fair-Weather Friend? Dealing with the Mother-in-Law You're Dealt

She may throw her arms around you and welcome you into the family or she may tell him you're not what she expected. You can choose your husband but you can't choose your mother-in-law. Even if you have landed the grooviest guy on earth you have a slim chance she'll be groovy too. Whatever type of mother-in-law you've inherited here's the 411 on what's in store:

YOUR BEST BUDDY

Lucky lady, not only do you have an irresistible guy but you have a delightful mother-in-law to boot. As soon as she met wonderful you, she encouraged Your Guy to hold on to you. She knew a good woman, wife, and daughter-in-law when she saw one. When you got engaged, she cried with joy, gave you a family heirloom to mark the moment and popped open a bottle of bubbly she had waiting. When she introduces you as her daughter-in-law she will beam with pride. If she has only boys and no girls you're in luck, you'll be the beloved daughter she always wanted. She'll treat you to all the girly things she could never do with sons—oxygen facials, weekend spa getaways, and eight-hour-long shopping excursions. You hang out with her so often, your own mother is getting jealous. She's at the ready with marriage, career, or decorating advice, but only when asked. She respects your opinion and thinks you make a dynamite match for her precious son. You should be so lucky.

YOUR NIGHTMARE NEMESIS

You found Mr. Right but his mother is Mrs. Wrong. She will constantly say things like "Why do you do it *that* way?" or "I've never heard of such a thing." When you two announced your engagement she cried, but you don't think they were tears of joy. She will display photographs of family trips from years past that included Your Guy's ex-girlfriends. "Remember that summer Alana spent with us at the beach?" she'll ask Your Guy during dinner. She'll include you by saying, "You didn't know Alana, but she was lovely." She will feign innocence if called on those remarks. The only pics of you in the house are wedding photos where you've got your eyes closed but she and Your Guy look fab. When she refers to your taste as extravagant, bold, or unique know that she really means overdone, tacky, and hideous. When you talk about your career she will say things like "Things are so different these days. In my day you weren't selfish, you got married and made kids your priority." She will buy you presents with hidden meanings, or lend you a copy of that depressing book about how, as a baby maker, it's all downhill for you after age twenty-seven. She will bring you cookbooks even if you've told her you hate cooking. If this is your fate, good luck to you. Here's your chance to put the advice of Mexican shaman Don Miguel Ruiz to work: "Don't take it personally." Not even Alana would have made Mommie Dearest happy.

FAIR WEATHER IN-LAW

You've landed a mother-in-law who may be marvelously kind or even notoriously divaesque. Either way, she floats in and out of your lives when it suits her purpose. If she's a famous star she may ring you guys up for photo shoots and charity parties to project the domestic image her PR people want. But most of the time she leaves you two lovebirds alone. She can't be counted on for much, which has its pros and cons. When you have kids she won't be babysitting, but she will toss you a luxurious baby shower. She might forget to call Your Guy on his birthday, but she will send him a big check. Since she's only around part time, the time she's around she's always on overdrive. Count on her to celebrate the good times with you and vanish onto some tropical island when you're going through bad times. You can always expect a postcard.

Meeting and Eventually Winning Over His Parents

Your best friend, Olivia, was always loved and adored by the parents of her steady boyfriends. Sean's mother (Sean was Olivia's dorky boyfriend from college), actually sobbed when they broke up. She seemed more attached to Olivia than to Sean. Olivia's mother's friends were always "dropping by" with their sons in tow. Most parents knew a good potential daughter-in-law when they saw one and Olivia was considered ideal. She was funny and outgoing, sporty and smart, not to mention extremely generous and helpful. What more could they ask for?

Then Olivia fell in love with Internet Guy. Whatever the rest of her friends thought, she knew he was The One right after that first smooch (he felt the same way and instant messaged her the next day to pre-propose). But Olivia's meeting with his parents wasn't love at first sight. While Olivia's parents were open and loving, Internet Guy's parents were reserved and formal. Olivia's night gig singing in a band puzzled and alarmed them. Talkative Olivia became tongue-tied around them for fear that they would disapprove of what she had to say.

After the wedding Olivia decided she was going to do everything she could to really bond with them. Her parents were crazy about IG and she wanted his parents to love her the same way. She tried showering them with gifts! They thought she was too extravagant. She tried cooking them her specialty, vegetarian dinner! Her father-in-law declared he was a meat and potatoes guy. She tried telling them about her promotion! Her mother-in-law wanted to hear about her (nonexistent) pregnancy.

IG insisted that they loved her, they just had a different way of expressing (or not expressing) their feelings. He suggested that she try and talk to them on their level. So Olivia brought out a baby name book and debated possible baby names with his mom (she didn't mention the baby would have to wait four years to be named). She went to the butcher with her father-in-law and picked out some T-bone steaks and asked for a lesson in working the grill. And it worked. While they never did gush about their love for her, they did invite her over—not to toast to her promotion but her anniversary with Internet Guy. A family picture with Olivia beaming in the middle appeared on the mantle. And his mother knit her a baby sweater for whenever Olivia was ready.

Locate Your Allies: The Secret to Surviving a New Family

Even if you get along famously with Your Guy, have friends that are hipper than *Friends*, a career that's speeding ahead like a car thief on the interstate, and a pad that's ready for a photo shoot, it's not enough. For a Thoroughly Modern Married Girl's life to sail smoothly, she also needs to vibe with his family. Being the cause of, or taking part in, huge family brawls is so *Jerry Springer*. Better to follow *Oprah*'s loving view of the universe and accept this interesting cast of characters as part of life's infinite mystery. Figuring out where you fit in is the next step. Don't feel like you have to be best buds with every member of his clan, just locate a few trusty allies and you're set for a lifetime of family reunions.

At family powwows, hang out with the relatives you love (his mischievous grandmother who gives you the dirt on everyone) and avoid the relatives you aren't wild about (his gambling maniac Uncle Mervin who placed bets on your marriage). Bond with your sister-in-law, who's already been through everything you're about to experience. She'll give you the scoop on what mistakes not to make (getting drunk at family parties) and how to endear yourself to your mother-in-law (prevent your father-in-law from getting drunk at family parties).

Allies are key, they give you the real deal on family dynamics, and support you when you're in a bind. You'll also have someone interesting to chat with at holidays other than Your Guy (who will be busy making the rounds). The sooner you spot relatives who are on your side, the less you'll actively dread family visits. If there's no one you have anything remotely in common with, play with the dog. No dog? Playing a game of hide-and-seek with the tots is a clever way to avoid family conversations but still get points for being so fantastic with the little ones.

The In-Law Slumber Party

You thought that moving across the country meant starting off on your own without family obligations and a pesky mother-in-law insisting you come for dinner every Sunday night, or else. But it's a trade-off. If you live within driving distance of your relatives, you will never get a call from them saying, "We're coming to stay for ten days, get the extra room ready!"

The reality of your own or his flesh and blood staying in your eight-hundred-square-foot apartment presents a few potential problems. The biggest is that you've got to spiff everything up including yourselves. Otherwise your trip will be filled with concerned family members trying to fix things that you two don't consider flaws. From a distance the clans are free to project whatever images they have on your life. They didn't know that you work sometimes until 11 P.M., that you can't cook anything except for toast (even that's iffy), and that Your Guy owns two Harleys. You would never lie to your in-laws or your parents, but you don't need to overwhelm them with the cold truth the day they arrive. So feel free to "cook" a dinner for them that's really from the gourmet shop on the corner. Just get rid of the containers and dirty lots of pots and pans heating it up. Throw a little food around on the countertop so no one gets suspicious. Take off a little early from work so your mother won't worry that she'll never be a grandmother. Keep the Harleys in the garage. The truth will come out eventually, but what's the hurry?

A smart MG makes lots of plans for their stay. She recruits friends (the presence of strangers will put family on their best behavior), and plans a packed two weeks that involve lots of activities. The busier you are with your in-laws doing sightseeing, walking tours, biking tours, boat tours, bus tours, and trolley tours, the better. Downtime will only result in catching-up time. And for your mother-in-law catching up will mean asking you when you are going to buy a place close by so she can see you every day.

Family Tug-of-War: Where Is Home for the Holidays?

A major holiday arrives and everyone wants you to come on over. You two are always in demand since you do jazz up any gathering, not to mention are masters at soothing any family tension that may arise. In true mom fashion your mother just assumes that you'll be with your family. His mother calls and tries to reserve you two for the shindig at her house. And not to be ignored, his stepmother sends you guys an email to see if you're free. It's good to be loved, but it makes things more complicated.

You and Your Guy both figured you'd spend the vacation at your respective places. Your trip home always involved arguing with your little sister over who got to put the star on the tree to the yearly soundtrack of your mom's *Bluegrass Christmas* and Kenny G's Holiday Album. On Your Guy's side, holidays involved shuttling between his mom's house to his dad and stepmother's house, and thoughtfully claiming that the other party was the pits. He could count on fabulous presents from his stepmother who's trying to win him over (still) and carving the usually overdone turkey.

Now that you're hitched, you've got to balance creating new traditions with honoring the ones that are indelibly stamped into your little holiday heart. If Your Guy hails from a different culture or faith, you have it easy. For Chinese New Year you go to his house and for Kwanzaa, he comes to yours. But for those of you whose families celebrate on the same day and expect you to toast to the holiday with them, you have more options than you think. Here are a few ideas:

GO TO BOTH

Everybody wins! You won't miss out on the all-night cocktail hour and deviled eggs at his parents pad and he'll get to eat Tofurkey and a chance to try Ashtanga yoga at your family's holistic holiday. If you live within realistic driving distance (thirty minutes or less) of both families, then go to both. Have one family host a lunch and the other host a dinner. If they both insist on a dinner then explain that only one of them will see you. You'll find this makes them instantly more flexible.

BE THE HOSTS

Invite everyone to your place! Include his single mom, his dad, his dad's girlfriend and their baby, as well as your clan. You've got the home court advantage, so not only does everyone have to behave but they have to do things your way. You guys can create your own entirely new, possibly irreverent, traditions. If you want to listen to MTV's Christmas album, eat Chinese takeout, and create twelve-step crafts from *Martha Stewart Living*, you can!

ALTERNATE

Tough choices have to be made. One year you go to his family's place and the next year he goes to yours. Be prepared that it might feel weird to spend a holiday with someone else's family. Everything is so different, even the tension. You'll also feel nostalgic for things you didn't expect to miss, like that *Bluegrass Christmas* album and your little brother's dirty jokes.

CELEBRATE ON A DIFFERENT DATE

If you do decide to alternate, you'll have to deal every year with one disappointed family. You can, of course, choose to live with the guilt. Or you can try to make everyone happy (key word being "try"). To appease the clan that you aren't with on the big day, celebrate with them on a different date, like celebrating Christmas on the twenty-sixth. If you do this, make a point to be as jazzed up as if your festivities were taking place on the actual date. Get dolled up, put on the holiday tunes, and get in the spirit.

Staying in Your In-Laws' Good Graces After the Wedding

Don't slack off on impressing your in-laws after the deal is sealed. Stay in their good graces by following these tricks gleaned from MGs whose in-laws adore them:

- Even after you say "I do" and they can't veto you anymore, continue to write gushing thank-you notes. Whether it's a birthday present or a weekend stay, show appreciation with a gracious card. Even after they tell you that you're not obligated to write one, write it anyway. No one does this anymore so yours will certainly be the only handwritten note in their mailbox.

- Scope out everyone's secret weakness, whether it be for Andrea Bocelli CDs or those miniature chocolate bottles filled with whiskey, and bring them on your visits. It's impossible to dislike someone who knows your soft spots.

- Prepare forty-six conversational gambits in advance. Or at least have a number of questions to ask, beyond "What have you been up to?" because the answer will inevitably be "Not much."

- Ask to see the family movies—again. Laugh, again, and be moved, again.

- Offer to take the kids to the zoo, the park, or wherever. Hey, you're out of the house! You'll also score points with your brother- and sister-in-laws for giving them a moment of calm.
- Learn something new that only they can teach you. If his dad loves the horses ask him to explain the art of handicapping. Ask a million questions and time flies. Just don't ask him while he's watching the Kentucky Derby.

CHAPTER FOUR

Your Friends and Neighbors: Getting Along with the World Outside Your House

Planet of the Couples

If you're not careful, once you're married Saturday nights can take on a whole new vibe. You may suddenly find yourself making the rounds of couples potluck suppers and playing Pictionary when you formerly played strip poker and let loose at wild singles bashes. In this alternate couples universe everything from hobbies to vacations is all about being a duo. Activities like couples bowling tournaments, mixed doubles tennis tournaments, and group couples getaways to Mexican spas can take the place of singles meet-and-greet bowling nights, bar crawls, and Club Med. There are advantages to the Planet of Pairs. You no longer have to deal with some creepy Casanova asking if you were in *Playboy* last month. Instead you'll have envious Married Girls asking if you were featured in the latest *Town & Country* weddings page.

Now that you're a ring-carrying member of the Couples Planet, haven't you noticed that married friends who had all but disappeared from your life have started inviting you two to play golf? It will be the same when you're preggers and your friends with babies suddenly want you to come over for tea and meet other new moms. It's all about comparing notes. Married Girls bond over swapping mother-in-law-from-hell stories the way single women trade tales of dates from hell. This is great (isn't it reassuring to know your friends are going through the same first-year issues you are?). But separate camps get set up, as people pair off, split up, and add little ones. They're the Singletons Planet, Couples Planet, Pregnant and Parenting Planet, and the Planet of the Divorcées. Avoid only interacting with people who are experiencing the same things as you—there is nothing deadlier! Only hanging out with other newly married couples breeds a terribly narrow, not to mention dull perspective. Don't get sucked into thinking there's a moving walkway through married life and you just got on it. While it's easy to land on the Planet of the Pairs and stay there until you're pregnant, it's better to expand your horizons. Offer to treat a pregnant friend to a pedicure, provide babysitting services for a new mom, and burn old photographs with your friend who's divorcing. The Thoroughly Modern Married Couple respects all forms of life, not just married life!

Couple Dating: Shopping for Friends You Both Like

You have a rock-solid group of beloved gal pals who have seen you through exam weeks, job interviews, and an engagement that wasn't meant to be. Your Guy has his own group of steady buddies that he went to camp, ran marathons, and lived with post-college while trying to make it in the big city. But when you add a boyfriend or wife to your best friends, or meet new couples, your social life gets a little trickier. As a pair you *both* have to like *both* people in a couple to want to socialize with them regularly. If one of you doesn't like one of them, chances are you won't be going to their lake house on weekends. So begins your shopping spree for other couples to be friends with (you definitely need a few). Here's a little glimpse of what to expect when socializing as a duo:

BEST BUDS

You're all four friends. Your Guy talks sports and compares husband notes with Her Guy and chats about the latest episode of CSI with her. She's smart, savvy and on your side and he's a career mentor for you. You feel like you can talk honestly about everything with them, including your marriage. "My Guy has been driving me bananas lately!" you can confess without worry that they will broadcast that info to some Impossibly Smug Married Couple. It's true couple friendship and hard to find.

BEST BUDS WITH ONLY HALF OF A PAIR

Your best friend, Olivia, married a guy who is a little geeky, antisocial, and obsessed with the Internet. He even has his own Web page where he chronicles the lives of his favorite celebrities as well as his life with Olivia (Olivia and he watching the Red Sox! He and Olivia swimming on South Beach! The two of them going jogging in matching outfits!). Neither you nor Your Guy is wild about Internet Guy. He's a PC and you're Macs. Even though you love hanging out with Olivia, it's a little difficult to rev up to spend your free time listening to him drone on about how Heather Locklear has over 1,576 fan websites (he's surfed every one) or that he saw a pre-release bootleg of the latest *Star Wars* flick online. You honestly wonder what Olivia sees in him. But since you absolutely adore Olivia, struggling through couple time with them every so often is a must. Being the sweet man that Your Guy is, he'll endure an evening or two with IG, but Your Guy and Internet Guy just don't vibe. Inevitably, the evening will end up with you and Olivia catching up in one corner while Your Guy makes awkward attempts at conversation with IG. Since Olivia is madly in love with Internet Guy she may not notice that he's boring everyone to tears or that you two avoid him. This is a good thing. You don't want Olivia to catch on, it will only hurt your friendship. The best way not to lose touch with Olivia is to plan a multitude of girls' nights with her: Pedicures! Feminist Plays! Pilates! Anything to get her out of the house, SOLO. Beware, unless you tell her that Your Guy is busy that night she will say, "Since we're going out why doesn't Your Guy come over and hang with My Guy?"

BEST BUDS WITH A SWORN SINGLE AND THEIR REVOLVING DOOR OF DATES

A Thoroughly Modern Married Girl remembers what it's like to be the new girlfriend meeting his couple friends, so even if some of your guy friends have dates who hail from bimboland, you try and bond. Your Guy's childhood friend Tom, for instance, has a habit of dating girls who think making it big would be a lingerie shot in a Macy's ad. Tom often calls you and Your Guy to go out since you give him an air of credibility. Tom's gals think that because he has normal married friends, Tom may also want to get married one day. Flawed logic. Since he's your husband's oldest friend, you make the best of evenings with Tom and The Babe of the Month. You hit it off with her and net crafty beauty tips and dishworthy celebrity gossip:

She'll tell you who the hot new hairstylist is, how to get your eye makeup to last, and who George Clooney is really dating. This expert info can come in handy. It's always good to know which bikini waxer to stay away from.

Making New Friends but Hanging On to Old Ones

Sometimes, marriage changes how even your close friends start to see you. They fear you've hopped on board the marriage express never to be fun again. Your friend Lola may stop inviting you to go out with her because she assumes you're busy with Your Guy. If you do invite her out she may decline, not wanting to be the third wheel with you two on a Saturday night (unless Your Guy has cute single buddies). In your attempts not to lose her you may think you can just set her up and have Lola join you on the couple side of things. "If you date My Guy's friend Chip then we can hang out as couples!" you may exclaim to her horror, giving her more proof that she never wants to get married. It's not really your fault, marriage is a little like a cult, you always want new recruits. Since you're so ecstatic being married you may want everyone else to hop on board the love train. But not everyone wants to join you in coupleland, they're perfectly happy swinging from the chandeliers and dating different people every weekend.

You certainly don't want to lose your loyal friend Lola as a casualty of marriage. Instead you need to do two things to stay on board with her. First, let her know that just because you're hitched doesn't mean you can't go out solo. You're always up for a good party. Second, incorporate her into your new life and some of the new friends that come along with it. Throw lots of dinner parties to bring everyone together. You won't have to feel guilty about making new friends when you bring old and new buddies together. Introduce Lola to some of your couple friends as well as some of your great girl friends from work. Of course, if she's on the prowl it doesn't hurt to invite Your Guy's cute single boss one week and your dashing dentist the next.

It Takes a Village to Make a Relationship

Since you have an instant playmate, running partner, and all-around fantastic friend in your husband, it's tempting to only do things as a duo. But for the Thoroughly Modern Couple to exist in bliss, they know that it takes a village to make a relationship. Yes, that means letting Your Guy run wild with his single buddies or bond solo with his brother. On your end it means not planning girls' nights only on evenings that Your Guy is booked. While your hubby is of primary importance in your life, don't make everyone else feel like second best.

Your friends and family are key players in your relationship. They keep you from becoming totally codependant and smothering each other. And they help keep it all in perspective. Not everyone has it so good in the love department and sometimes it's good to get a glimpse of that to appreciate what you've got. But one of the best parts of having an ensemble cast in your marriage play is that they take the pressure off of you two to be absolutely everything to each other. Now you don't have to sit through midnight shows at CBGB; Your Guy prefers going with Stan, his spiky-haired work friend. On the flip side, Your Guy is happy you've stopped inviting him to join your contemporary fiction book group, when he prefers Hemingway. Better to play to each other's strengths and rely on your friends to make up the difference.

Us Time vs. Party Time

You two have been invited to a work event on Monday, a coed baby shower on Tuesday, a dinner at Olivia's house Wednesday, a lecture on Thursday, parties Friday and Saturday, and a barbecue on Sunday. It's great to be popular. But you'll find at the end of the week you've been so busy socializing that you haven't had a second to catch up with each other. You know it's bad when you overhear Your Guy talking about his great new boss or his terrific job opportunity and it's the first you've heard of it.

As a Thoroughly Modern MG you don't ever feel guilty about sometimes saying no to great invitations because you two have a date lined up. You might miss a fun fete, but you can't be everywhere at once. Strike a balance between socializing time and us time, by scheduling nights together on the calendar. Mark the nights you're going to stay in, too; they're just as important as the nights you go out. When you were dating, your friends understood that a date was a date and they didn't expect you to break it. But now that you're married, people sometimes think that nights it's just the two of you are nights that you're free. Be elusive and just say you have "plans." No one needs to know your plans are to make out on the couch.

Casualties of Marriage: Saying Goodbye to Old Beaus and Bad Friends

When you tie the knot there will be a few people you'll break up with. Old flames, your male fan club, and superficial friends will all be ancient history. Certain friends have no interest in joining you on your journey into the world of Smug Marrieds, so you'll let them go. Here are a few sidekicks that may get kicked out of your inner circle:

YOUR SERIOUS EXES

Remember when you were breaking up with your beloved beau Skip and you vowed to be friends forever? Well, "forever" translated to "until one of us gets engaged." An old love is never really a friend anyway. There is always someone who wishes it wasn't over. Your ex Skip was either on the back burner if someone better didn't come along—a security blanket if your soulmate got stuck in traffic. Or Skip was the ex that you always imagined you would eventually end up with (once he grew up, got a job, and had that tattoo lasered off).

Now that you're married, it's time to say goodbye to Skip. There's really no room for him in your life anymore. Your best friend, dance partner, and sidekick are all spots that have been filled by Your Guy. With few exceptions, it's too much to ask Your Guy to continue a "friendship" with a man who was once your lover. No matter how studly, confident, and secure Your Guy is, it will always be on his mind that you once had a love life with Skip. After all, Skip has also spent weekends with your family, shared an apartment with you, and knows what you look like in the A.M. It's fairly impossible to try and make two men that have seen you naked into good friends.

There are two rare scenarios where you won't be saying goodbye to Skip. One, if he's part of your close social circle and you can't get away from each other. If Skip's on the scene you should be friendly, funny, and fabulous but not too friendly, too funny, or too fabulous or it will be translated as flirting. In this case expect Your Guy to be on a very superficial level with Skip. Don't expect him to invite him to play tennis (although he may want to invite him to a round of boxing). Two, if Skip gets married, then you can spend time as couples now that neither Your Guy nor Skip's wife is worried about you two getting back together. Most likely, however, Skip's wife won't want to be anywhere near you since you're the goddess that he never got over.

HIS TERRIBLE EXES

Fair's fair, and you don't really want Your Guy's serious exes hanging around either. Women are much more possessive than men, and ex-girlfriends won't be deterred by your engagement. They will want to be invited to the wedding. While most ex-boyfriends tend to get lost as soon as they know there are no more opportunities with you (your wedding is officially that point), ex-girlfriends are too invested to fade away gracefully. Exes want to get to know you, not because they want to be your friend, but because they want to know exactly what type of girl their Former Guy is ending up with. They see his choice of you as a marriage partner as some sort of reflection on them. "Ex-Guy never liked brunettes!" she'll say if she's blonde. It's a good sign to be with a man who doesn't say horrible things about his exes and whose exes don't think he is the devil incarnate. But there are limits. Your marriage is about looking toward your shared future, not about bringing along your separate baggage.

YOUR MALE FAN CLUB

As a captivating single girl you had a large following of male friends that you assumed would carry over into married life. There was Nelson, the short-lived beau who was a much better platonic friend. And George, who was madly in love with you but accepted "just friends," hoping you'd eventually capitulate and be his girlfriend someday. While many single men claim to be your friend, once there is a ring on your finger they won't be ringing you up anymore. No earth-shattering breakup, just him gradually drifting off into the single sea.

Most single men don't want to waste their free time hanging out with a Married Girl. You'll notice when you are chatting with a single guy, as soon as you say "my husband" he will flee almost immediately. It's not that men and women can't be friends, but you'll find that extremely close relationships with single, heterosexual members of the opposite sex are the exception not the norm. Unless your male friends are gay, you probably won't be going out alone for drinks, dinner, movies, or plays with them anymore. As an MG most of the unwed guys that you'll pal around with will be your girlfriends' beaus or Your Guy's entourage. Your Guy's single buddies will be your new Male Fan Club. Since you magically got their pal to walk down that long and dreaded aisle, they view you as some sort of love guru, and they'll want your take on their unsettled love lives. They'll be so grateful and admiring, in fact, that Your Guy will have to forgive them for having a little innocent crush on you.

BAD FRIENDS

Since you'll be spending a lot of your playtime with your man, you won't have heaps of extra time to socialize with people who don't matter to you. When you were single you were OK with hanging out with random groups because you never knew who you might meet. But now you don't want to waste time with hangers-on.

For example, your gorgeous model friend Lucille, who wanted a nonmodel friend so she would always look prettier, will probably not stick around. She'll head off to find another wing woman who will let her be the belle of the ball. Girlfriends who are all about men will also disappear. If you were great pals with boy-crazy Anne when you were both dating brothers, but now Your guy isn't in her guy's circle of friends, you won't be either.

THE MG FILES:

The Ex Files

He was my Mr. Big. Roberto was a few years older, beyond hand-some, and made me feel like the most clever and attractive girl on the planet. He also was a notorious womanizer, impossible to pin down, and as a result the LAST man I wanted to fall in love with. We only dated briefly (in retrospect he was also probably dating a few other people at the same time) and we kept in touch after the breakup. We'd meet up now and then to take samba lessons, go bowling, catch some jazz. I never fell in love with him, preferring in-stead to keep him at a safe distance (which is probably why he kept calling). I liked having him as a steady walker not as a boyfriend. I had all the benefits of his company but none of the heartbreak. He was always the one to call when I wanted to make some inattentive beau jealous or give my self-esteem a boost when there were no suit-ors around. After seven years, I considered him a fixture in my life that for better or worse I had grown awfully fond of.

When My Guy and I began to date, he didn't appreciate my re-lationship with the dashing Roberto. My Guy tried to act like he didn't care but would toss out passive-aggressive zingers like "I don't know why you waste time talking to that loser." He thought it was weird to have some older single ex as my "friend" As our ro-mance blossomed, I had little need for Roberto. My Guy was my studly and smart partner in crime now. Besides, after I went to a party of Roberto's without him, My Guy went for dinner with a

babelicious "friend" of his own. Point taken. When Roberto heard
through the grapevine of my impending nuptials he phoned not to
congratulate me but to say goodbye. I had just assumed we would
always be in touch, but he knew when to head for the door. "You've
got my number if it doesn't work out," he said laughing. "Too bad I
don't think you'll be calling." We haven't spoken a word since.

The Opposing Team: Impossibly Smug Married Girls

For the Thoroughly Modern Married Girl whose recipe for a happy
marriage is highly individual, the Impossibly Smug Married Girl is a
cruel nemesis always out to make trouble. She's obsessed with making her marriage look better than yours. She throws out odd, but cal-
culated, comments like "We never fight" or "Harvey makes all the
decisions and I wouldn't have it any other way." Going to college was
simply another scheme to nab a husband. If the Impossibly Smug
went on to get an MBA it was simply to increase her odds of finding a rich husband. Any friends she has came with her spouse, a gift-
with-purchase of sorts.

When you ask the Impossibly Smug how everything is, she will
boast about hot sex every night, her husband's lavish salary, amazing
real estate deals, and incredible jewels he just happened to pick up.
Be skeptical. She won't tell you anything about herself because her
whole life is her husband's. These women play a constant game of
Couple Smackdown, and they want to hold you down for a count of
three while they do the victory dance. The truth is Impossibly Smug

wants so much to be happily married that she thinks she has to prove your marriage is unhappy to get there.

Never reveal anything to Impossibly Smug or she will put a negative spin on it and broadcast it on CNN. For example, if you say something as innocent as "My Guy is just so busy with work I don't see him as much as I would like," she will tell everyone that he is having an affair with his sexy assistant and you two are splitsville. When confronted, the Impossibly Smug will say something cryptic like "You should really pay more attention to Your Guy." This statement is designed to cause minor anxiety attacks and distrust of Your Guy (who we all know is madly in love with you and only you). You could, if you wanted to, beat the Impossibly Smug at her own game. But you, being the kind, sensitive soul you are would only feel guilt, not delight, over making someone else miserable.

The way to deal with the Impossibly Smug is simple. Smile and nod your head the way you did when your mother told you not to wear pink lipstick because it didn't suit your skin tone (and then you bought three more tubes). Chances are you will have to deal with the Impossibly Smug even if you don't want to. She may be married to your husband's brother, she may sit in the cubicle next to yours, or she could be in the apartment across the hall. If this is the case, just accept her competitive ways as a compliment. If you weren't so damn terrific, she wouldn't be trying to one-up you all the time.

His Awful Buddies

A Thoroughly Modern Married Girl always encourages her guy to hang out with his friends. But when his friends are womanizing, beer-guzzling guys who love telling you about their sexcapades, you sometimes wish they weren't his friends. Wish all you want, but Your Guy is probably going to keep them in his social circle after "I do." The beer guzzlers who bring over funnels and always have porn in their briefcases probably don't want to hang out with you either, since you stole their partner in crime and made him yours. Since he's got to hang out with them, it's probably best that he do it solo.

When the friends cross the line and show up on your date night with play-off tickets, they put you in a bad spot (and they know it). Say no and you look like a possessive wife. Say yes and you're left dateless wearing a cocktail dress. He may even have friends who like to tell you how "incredibly attractive" you are. Yuck. Let Your Guy handle this stuff on his own. You didn't sign on to be Yoko to his band of buddies, so let him be the one to tell them when they've gone too far. If you tell them, they might even enjoy it.

Couple Competitions: How to Avoid Trying to Keep Up with the Joneses

You're out for sushi and sake with a group. An Impossibly Smug Married Girl and her guy are across the table. You and Your Guy have just bought an apartment that you love, you're giving the details to the crowd. "It's adorable," you begin and Impossibly Smug interrupts, "Oh, we looked at your place before we had any idea what we wanted. It was way too small for us, but such a steal." She will then go on to talk about her humungous apartment and it's accoutrements. She has reduced your terrific first pad to a cheap, tiny place that wasn't good enough for the likes of her.

Do you compete back? Do you point out that your husband is Brad Pitt's body double? Do you toss out that you're about to get your dual PhD in neuroscience and political science?

NO.

A smart Married Girl doesn't fall into her trap. If someone wants to be the star, let them. From proposal stories, salaries, neighborhoods, brand of cars, brilliance and attractiveness of babies, to brilliance and carats of jewels, the Impossibly Smugs want to compete with you.

So uncool. The Thoroughly Modern Married Girl never wastes time thinking about what material things she doesn't have (emerald cocktail ring and expense account at Saks) instead of what she does (faithful man who loves her to pieces and an earth-shattering sex life). She is competitive only with herself. Who wants to keep up with the Joneses? Since you two are so terrific, the Joneses are probably trying to keep up with you. Life and marriage are not like a ferris wheel, that in order to be up someone else has to be down. As a wonderful couple you are never threatened by anyone else's success, instead you applaud it. And when someone is threatened by your success you let it go. When the Impossibly Smug Married Girl boasts about her spiffy pad while putting down yours, ask her when you can come over and visit. Bring her a really marvelous house-warming present.

How to Stay Together Through Your Friends' Divorce

Your closest friends, Harry and Mabel, got married the year before you and Your Guy. Your Guy was the best man at their wedding. During his toast Your Guy talked about how Harry was a serial heart-breaker until he met Mabel. But under Mabel's blue-eyed gaze, Harry wanted nothing more than to be her husband and proposed on the second date. All the guests at the wedding sighed dreamily while watching them float across the dance floor. If any couple was meant to be, it was Harry and Mabel.

Harry and Mabel's love was infectious, Your Guy proposed soon after their wedding. They were your role models for a happy marriage. They never fought, always backed each other up, and talked endlessly of having a large family. Now, two years later, they tell you they're over. Splitsville. You don't understand how it's possible. They seemed so perfect that you sometimes had a complex being around them. With all that PDA and googly eyes, you felt like prudes. It just didn't work out, they try and explain to you. They didn't really know what love was, they had a fling with a coworker, they wanted to have a fling with a coworker, they don't believe in marriage anymore, they never really loved each other, they think they would be better off as friends.

WHAT?

What about soulmates? What about true love? What about till death do you part? What about *our* marriage?

In the months that follow, their split becomes less amicable. Mabel tells you of a brilliant and booby flame-haired lawyer whom she suspects Harry was cheating on her with. Harry tells Your Guy about how Mabel only married him for his money. You take Mabel's side and flash Harry dirty looks when you see him. Your Guy, of course, sides with Harry. The battle lines are drawn in your own house as well. You obsess over every detail they give you, and anything that compares with your own marriage makes you extraordinarily uncomfortable. You barrage Your Guy with questions: Are you attracted to brainy redheaded lawyers with huge boobs? Do you think this will ever happen to us? He lovingly, calmly, and sweetly settles your fears. It never occurs to Your Guy that what's happening to Mabel and Harry would ever happen to you. Despite his calming words you still can't sleep. You wake him up at 3 A.M. to ask if he believes in divorce. You make him vow not to turn you in for a younger sexier model when you're wrinkled and cranky after years of chasing after your screaming children.

It will be even more bizarre when you see Mabel or Harry happy again. It throws off your sense of what's real and what's not. When Mabel becomes the dashing divorcée and Harry the swinging single, they may want to make marriage seem like the pits. Know that *their* marriage was the pits, not marriage itself. At some point you will claim custody of one of the two warring spouses. It's almost impossible to be friends with both of them. Mabel will know that you have gone out for dinner with Harry and the redhead. She will be hurt and try and pump you for information. Harry will know that you have been listening to Mabel's version of events. He will be defensive. They both want you to side with them and divorce the other person.

Watching your friends split up makes you not only sad for them, but aware of the vulnerabilities in your own marriage. Seeing them with a new mate is worse, it makes you feel replaceable. Yet, after you are over comparing yourselves, you will realize, first, that you can never really know what goes on in someone else's marriage. The face they give to the world isn't necessarily the truth. The constantly bickering couple may turn out to be a tougher duo than the couple who pretends everything is roses. Second, you will be reminded of how fragile marriage is. It's never perfect. It needs lots of attention. Little problems have a way of multiplying like rabbits if they aren't dealt with when they arrive. It's a wake-up call from the fantasyland of young marriage.

Hanging Out with Singletons Without Wanting to Go Back

Your nights out now with the singletons have a decidedly different tone than when you were part of the singles scene. Now that you know who you're going home with, evenings are quite a bit less dramatic than before. No more first kisses, waiting for phone calls, and wondering if that stud who just walked trough the door will be your next beau. So when you're out with the girls and the talk turns to your friend Claire's date with the sexy photographer and her week-end in London with her old flame, you may think your life isn't quite as exciting. You also may feel like you have nothing to add when the convo steers inevitably away from politics to the juicy business of dating. Everyone just assumes everything is perfect with you and will ask a quick "How's Your Guy?" You're expected to keep up with the happily-ever-after fantasy and answer with "Everything's great." Then the conversation will turn back to your friends' dating es-capades and you can easily feel left out, a boring old married broad. You remember feeling wistful when you were solo and everyone seemed to be getting engaged. You never thought you would mourn your single self.

Now that you're married your life lacks the drama of your single life. You used to talk about every detail with your friends: "I wouldn't let him into my apartment so we kissed goodnight for three hours on my doorstep!" or "He sent me an email that said 'I hope to see you around.' Is that a good or bad sign?" When you were dating you dis-cussed your relationship's every nuance, every zinger, every smooch, every word of love or hate with your friends. Now that you're an MG, disclosing those details feels like you're betraying your hus-band. You have to edit your revelations or they will think you're mar-ried to a jerk. The last thing you want to go around is "She's great but her husband's such a loser." Sure, tell your girlfriends when he's slightly grumpy or when you had a dynamite date, but not the same in-depth postgame wrap-up as before. You certainly wouldn't call another MG and say, "You won't believe the sex we had last night!" Now you're a little more coy, when talk turns to sex you just say, "I'm a very lucky woman."

Single girls have a fantasy world where marriage seems to be perfect and married girls have a fantasy world where single life seems to be so carefree. But keep listening, Claire may have gotten back from her sexy date and never heard from the photographer again, and her old flame may have just proposed to her old friend. You'll remember only too well the heartbreak of dating. After a few tales of "unhappily ever after" all you will want to do is crawl in bed with Your Guy and thank your lucky stars. And when you're in bed together, you'll also remember that stability isn't quite so boring after all.

MARRIED LIFE ON THE SILVER SCREEN

Hollywood likes to finish dating flicks with "happily ever after." But Tinseltown's take on marriage is sometimes more of a horror show. They love to show rampant affairs, killer mistresses, and lonely housewives. Thankfully, they've produced a few romance flicks about the road to true love. Here are the messages of movies that inspire us on our journey to lifetime bliss and others that make us hang on to our husbands!

MG LOVE STORIES	MG HORROR STORIES
When Harry Met Sally The best husband is your best friend.	**Fatal Attraction** Blond, smart, psycho, and after your man, an MG's worst nightmare.
The Wedding Singer Proof that marrying the dorky guy who's wild about you is the way to go.	**Unfaithful** Unhappily Ever After. Even if he's a beyond-sexy French guy with a killer bod, happiness doesn't lie in someone else's bed.
Moonstruck Moral of the story: never marry a guy who loves his	**Husbands and Wives** Woody Allen's view of marriage always involves young

mother more than you. Only marry the guy that is crazy in love with you, even if that means he's a little crazy.

My Big Fat Greek Wedding

Opposites attract and love conquers all (even marrying into each other's quirky families).

The Princess Bride

Fairy tales can come true. Of course they also involve marrying the wrong guy and fake deaths, but then comes "happily ever after."

babes who want to sleep with neurotic middle-aged men. Well, it worked for him.

The Way We Were

Opposites attract, but love doesn't conquer all.

My Best Friend's Wedding

Proof that it's never a good idea to make Your Guy's "best friend" your maid of honor unless you want her to try and steal your man and wreck your wedding.

CHAPTER FIVE

Party Time

The Hosts with the Most:
Entertaining 101

Since the registry gods blessed you with enough stemware for a mob, it's time to christen your new wares by throwing your first shindig as a dynamic duo. Your friends shelled out their hard-earned cash, and they're rightfully demanding to see their wedding presents in action. So light up your new Weber, pull out your monogrammed cocktail napkins, and have a party. Whether you want to throw a sophisticated soiree or a blowout, it's all in setting the vibe ahead of time, keeping your cool, and, most important, sweating it out together.

BE AN EARLY BIRD

Starting off the evening with Your Guy stalling your guests at the door, while you shout, "They're here? Already?" doesn't set a party vibe. As an entertaining goddess, the MG knows that when you open the door you two should be ready to get down and enjoy the party (not trying to clean off the salad dressing and chopped onion that's stuck in your hair). The key to banishing the frantic stress of pulling it all together by the time your first friend arrives lies in prep work that starts the week before. The MG's entertaining mantra? Never let them see you sweat.

THE WEEK BEFORE: Stock up on tea lights, ice, bottles of bubbly, matches, and other party provisions. Take inventory well before the event to figure out what you forgot (there's always something). It sure beats sending Your Guy out during cocktail hour to buy wine glasses.

THREE NIGHTS BEFORE: Set the scene. Set the table and line up the votives. Clean your martini glasses, pull out the Moroccan lanterns, put salt in the salt shaker. If your tablecloth has a huge red wine stain that can't be covered by a vase full of tulips, you'll have time to get it cleaned.

TWO NIGHTS BEFORE: Tonight, clean, organize, and style your pad rather than desperately throwing everything under the bed fifteen minutes before your guests' prying eyes arrive. Neatening up will prevent the accidental display of an embarrassing item or two like your dog-eared copy of the *Kama Sutra* or his floor-strewn tighty whities.

THE NIGHT BEFORE: Save yourselves from a migraine or two by choosing dishes you can cook tonight and heat up the day of. Food that can be served cold is even better since it goes from fridge to sideboard.

THE DAY OF: If you do decide that you must cook the day of the fete, choose low-maintenance dishes. An MG believes cooking should be as low maintenance as possible, but it doesn't hurt if dishes are so amazing they give the illusion you're a pro. No-fuss dishes that can be left unattended in the oven beat tricky stir-fries, reduction sauces, and sautés. To make things even simpler, follow the TV cooking show example by chopping, slicing, and pureeing all the ingredients and setting them out in little bowls before you get to cooking. Martha would be proud.

COOK UP SOMETHING NEW

Supposedly, you shouldn't cook a new dish for the first time when you're expecting guests. But are you really going to make herb-rubbed rack of lamb or lobster potpie for just the two of you? Maybe not. Parties are the time to pull out the showstoppers, and sometimes that means trying a dish that *sounds* fabulous. If you're going to risk it all on a recipe you've never made before, have a backup plan you can pull out in a jiffy. Your friends aren't going to be upset if your meal didn't work out and you order Chinese takeout. You never know, your guests might even prefer a good Peking duck to the mushy mushroom risotto you usually make. However, when you're cooking dinner for your mother-in-law, your boss, or someone less forgiving (like an Impossibly Smug Married Girl), better stick to an old standby recipe that works every time.

GO WITH THE FLOW

A host and hostess who are stressing out rather than enjoying themselves kill their own party. Go with the flow and the party will follow. When something does go wrong your guests will be looking to you two to set the tone. If you're having a blast and laughing off any entertaining emergencies, your guests will too. At a certain point you have to give up control to the party gods and have a good time. Ignore that piece of brie on the floor, the wine glass rings on your coffee table, and your friend Alex who is rudely interrupting people. After all, a gathering is supposed to be about fun and friends, not about stressing over a burnt turkey or Your Guy's embarrassing friend Larry, who is drowning in scotch and asking people how much money they make. It's impossible to put out every fire and sometimes things get cooking when things go awry. Tomorrow, your friends won't be using their cell minutes to chat about your homemade crab cakes but re-hashing Harry's reaction to seeing his ex, Mabel, with her trophy husband.

USE YOUR FRIENDS

Every chef has a sous chef and so should you two. When your friend Eliza offers to bring her heavenly angel food cake or Jim mentions he blends a mean margarita, happily accept. A little potluck goes a long way. Just avoid hitting up the same people every time or an invitation to your house will always seem like work. If none of your guests offered to help out, even after you dropped a million and two hints, you're on your own. Calling up Olivia demanding she make her killer homemade apple pie when she hasn't offered will just start a cold war. Above all, never make honored guests sing for their supper. If you're throwing a shower for Your Guy's sister and she wants to bring something, just tell her to only bring her fabulous self.

USE YOUR GUY

The best way to look cool the day of is to put Your Guy on KP. Choose a dish that you don't know how to cook but your husband does. That way Your Guy will *have* to be in charge of cooking up his specialty. You may end up with bacon cheeseburgers and pigs in a blanket, but at least you won't be wilting away sweating over a hot stove.

CALL IN THE EXPERTS

Whether you're sneaking in a few courses from the corner gourmet food store or calling a caterer and claiming her goodies as your own, it's your party and you can lie if you want to. It's not cheating when you add store-bought divine dips to your soiree and accept the compliments. If the local caterer makes an incredible gazpacho that looks homemade, why not treat your guests to her delicacy? And this time let Your Guy take the credit. If entertaining is just not your thing or you don't have a nanosecond to pull off a spectacular soiree, a caterer goes a long way to making your party the talk of the town (and, trust me, it won't cost as much as the wedding). You'll feel like guests at your own party. The best part? At the end of the night the caterer handles the cleanup, and you and Your Guy can snuggle and dish about your stress-free bash. All you two had to do was look glam and circulate.

Throwing a Party Together

What's the fun of throwing a shindig, if only one of you does all the work? Many guys grew up watching their mothers prepare every bit of food, arrange every flower, pour every drink, chat up every guest, and clean every last plate while their dads hung out and smoked cigars. These guys think that parties happen magically, and the magicians are their wives. They won't ever say out loud that your job is to do all the work, but just watch. You two decide to have a shindig and Your Guy assumes buying ice and vodka is a big contribution to the event. Sorry boys. The Thoroughly Modern Married Girl knows that hosting a party together means planning, preparing, and throwing a party together.

GUERRILLA ENTERTAINING

Entertaining is a breeze when it's a team effort. As a duo you two can attack party planning like ninjas, whipping through the prep work together. Divide the party preparations by specialty. Whoever is the most skilled in the kitchen should attack the cooking while the other spouse dives into tunes, décor, and cocktails. Ideally you end up only doing what you like (making homemade sushi) and not what you don't (carting cases of wine up the stairs). One person cooks, the other cleans. One of you hits Chinatown, the other person hangs the paper lanterns and fills the noodle bowls. You play DJ, he gets people boogying.

YOUR REMEDIAL PARTY GUY

Entertaining isn't a breeze when only one of you knows how to entertain. If Your Guy thinks parties should revolve around TV sports and Bud, you have to teach him a few tricks. Start simple. If Your

Guy doesn't know the difference between a frying pan and a roasting pan and you send him to Stop & Shop alone, you'll get twenty desperate calls with questions like "What's arugula?" and "Is tahini a fruit?" Better to go along with him, split the grocery list in half, and hand him a walkie-talkie. When he's at a loss in the bread section ("What's the difference between twelve-grain and seven-grain?") you're only an aisle or two away to come to his rescue. In the kitchen, start him off with boiling water, chopping onions, and spinning salad. Giving him a recipe for raspberry chocolate mousse cake and expecting it to work out is wishful thinking. If pulling a party together results in a major shouting match or you both think of the kitchen as extra storage space for books, see "Call in the Experts" above. Parties should be fun! Remember?

How to Throw a Thoroughly Modern Cocktail Party

As couples in your crowd pair off, the standard for a successful party is no longer the random hook-up. So food, wine, and atmosphere have to go a long way to compensate. It's time to graduate from beer and nachos to mojitos and hot crab dip. Here are tips for sophisticated (but still sassy) party planning:

THE GUEST LIST

SOPHISTICATED: No need to prove how popular you are by inviting everyone you've ever said hi to. Being exclusive makes an invitation to your house more coveted. Better to assemble an interesting crowd even if it's on the small side. A few years ago you wouldn't have dreamed of inviting your older boss, your parents, or even your tattletale sister for fear they would be horrified by your wild ways (they would have been). Now you include anyone (even family) from twenty-one to one hundred and one, provided you think they're groovy.

SASSY: Feel free to cause a little innocent trouble with the guest list. Invite the cute guy at the office *and* the cute guy at Your Guy's office so you'll have some hunks for your divorcée pal Mabel to flirt with. Been having problems with your neighbors? Rather than hear them complain about the noise level, invite them to come and contribute to it at the bash.

INVITES

SOPHISTICATED: After you've got the guests down, shoot off a written invite a couple of weeks in advance. Email makes it too casual. Email says guests don't have to RSVP, can show up late, can bring random friends, come only if they feel like it, no big deal if they forget their deodorant. Written invites say make a fuss, it's the soiree of the season, put on a jazzy outfit, shine your shoes, get a blow-out, and be prepared for a good time.

SASSY: Send out an offbeat invite. Hip retro-print cardboard coasters, homemade CDs with party-theme songs, or a minibottle of bubbly all say let's get this party started.

DRESS CODE

SOPHISTICATED: Somewhere on the invite write the dress code (though if you say cocktails most people will know to spiff up a little). Specifying cocktail attire on the invite hopefully will prevent women from showing up in Britney Spears–inspired belly-baring tanks (might be impossible to avoid in LA) or guys arriving in sweatpants that bear the name of their favorite sports team.

SASSY: Set a theme. If your birthday's on the same day as Marilyn's have a bombshell fête complete with men in tuxes, champagne, and lots of diamonds (at least rhinestones). Or to celebrate your pairing, your theme can be Notorious Couples. Guests can dress up like Bonnie and Clyde, or solo blondes can come as Trump exes Ivana and Marla.

LENGTH

SOPHISTICATED: Setting a time for your cocktail party, six to eight, is a good idea in theory, but you will always have partiers who want the party to last all night. Having a late-night meeting spot will guarantee that everyone is out by nine-thirty, let's say. Have Your Guy spread the word that people are meeting up at "X" bar at ten. Then as ten approaches you can all head for the door. It also helps to run out of booze. As soon as you're short of vino your late-night guests will be on to the next spot.

SASSY: Hey, as long as you're up for it, if everyone's having a good time and wants to stay until sunrise, let 'em.

FOOD AND DRINK

SOPHISTICATED: If you're throwing an after-work cocktail party, most folks won't have fueled up on food beforehand. So serve some substantive and creative hors d'oeuvres. Otherwise, after a few measly crackers and a couple of tiny grapes, your friends will either leave early in search of sustenance or get bombed and stay all night.

SASSY: Choose a signature cocktail for the evening, make a pitcher or two and then let people mix their own drinks. That way you're free to chat. As for food, keep it easy. Order gourmet pizza and slice it in small pieces for an instant appetizer.

Party 911

Dining disasters and entertaining emergencies are going to strike. Whether it's a friend who's had way too much bubbly or an unexpected guest, you've got to keep the party moving and handle the potholes with finesse.

When friends arrive twenty minutes early, act like you expected them to arrive then, hand them a cocktail, and put them to work doing something painless like lighting candles or picking out tunes. They'll be a lot more comfortable lending a hand than standing around while you race around the apartment trying to finish up all the party prep.

One of your guests is an hour and a half late for dinner? She's missing a good time. Never let the food get cold and your guests get sloppy by waiting around for tardy Tanya. Start without her, but have a plate in the oven to pull out as soon as she steps through the door. Greet her with a "So happy to see you!" instead of growling about how she threw off the whole evening. Extra guests? Pull up some chairs and cook a side of pasta or warm another loaf of bread to cover the extra appetites. You find out a guest is a strict vegetarian when you're serving sirloin? Make the soup or salad appetizer their main course. One of your guests has a strict no-fat, no-carb, no-calorie diet? Serve them lettuce. Someone arrives in jeans and a ripped shirt when the invite said black tie? Who cares? When something spills, laugh it off and grab some club soda. When something breaks, pull out the Dustbuster rather than bursting out into tears and demanding payment. Your chicken is rubbery, pasta is overdone, or the grilled salmon is charred? Order pizza. Your guests would rather enjoy a slice and chuckle about dining disasters than watch you freak out. Something tastes terrible? Serve it to the dog.

GROOVIN' TUNES—WHAT TO PLAY FOR
COCKTAILS, DINNER, DANCING

Avoid killing the party mood with Gregorian chants when you should be spinning disco. Every party has a vibe, provided you've got the right tunes. Whether you're throwing a holiday party or frolicking by the pool, you've got to pick tunes that get the party started. Here are a few standbys to get you through a basic cocktail or dinner party. For dancing late night, pull out music that will have even the stodgiest guests boogying down.

Cocktails: Aretha Franklin, The Gypsy Kings, the Rat Pack, Hôtel Costes mixes, Buddha Bar mixes

Dinner: Frank Sinatra, Buena Vista Social Club (Omara Portuondo), India Arie, Angélique Kidjo, Ella Fitzgerald

Dancing: Use your own judgment. An MG's dance moves are her own prerogative.

COOL COCKTAILS

Every party should have a signature cocktail that's fun but also grown-up. Leave the frat-boy kegs and girlie Seabreezes behind and serve a creative but sophisticated drink for every season.

Winter: Toast to the holidays with a **French 75.** It's very potent so beware, but it's delicious and bubbly. Shake ½ ounce gin, ½ ounce Cointreau, and ¾ ounce fresh lemon juice with ice and pour into a champagne flute. Top with chilled champagne.

Spring: Try a **Thoroughly Modern** cocktail. Shake 2 ounces Stoli Rasberry vodka with 2 ounces of Absolut Mandarin, 2 ounces cranberry juice, juice of half a lime, and 1 ounce orange juice with ice and pour into a martini glass rimmed with sugar. Divine!

Summer: Cosmopolitans are so last season. **Caipirinhas** are a much cooler option for your garden party. Try this Brazilian favorite. Cut 4 lime wedges and put them in the bottom a glass. Add 2 tablespoons sugar and crushed ice. Blend and muddle, then add 2 ounces Cachaca

Fall: Heat things up with a **Moscow Mule** (I know, the name is so dorky, but it's good). Pour 2 ounces of vodka into a highball filled

with ice. Add the juice of two limes and ginger beer (not ginger ale)
and stir.

Secrets of a Successful Dinner Party

You've gathered an interesting and inspiring group together at your
place, but it's not exactly going according to plan. Tanya and Dan are
having an all-out battle over abortion rights, therefore endangering the
safety of your new wine glasses. Shelly, the smartest person in the
group, isn't talking but simply nodding her head in the direction of
several conversations she's not really listening to. Rachel and Rebecca
are gossiping over Ralph, who sits sullenly between them playing with
his linguine. You and Your Guy are trying to resuscitate the night,
which has turned into a major bomb. This disaster could have been
avoided with the right seating, the essential ingredient of any dinner
party: Ralph could be hitting it off with Tanya and planning their first
date for next Saturday. Dan could get Shelly to come out of her shell
and educate the rest of you on the pros and cons of the government's
international policies. Finally, Rachel and Rebecca, now separated,
could give everyone a dose of amusement by dishing their hot gossip
to the rest of the table. A good guest list and good seating, not food, not
décor, not your fabulous outfit, will make or break your dinner party.
So when you shell out the big bucks on pricey vino, a zillion varieties
of fresh flowers, and new Isaac slingbacks, be aware that nothing matters more than the right mix and the right placement of folks.

BE A PRIVATE EYE

Do a little background check on your guests before deciding who you're bringing together. A dinner of six to ten people is a fairly intimate affair, so avoid inviting former, but not current, friends and lovers. Just because these people love you and Your Guy doesn't mean they love hanging out with each other. Investigate who knows who as well as who does business with who. Just because Simon is Hally's stockbroker doesn't mean they want to socialize. Also, if Simon just lost several thousands of Hally's dollars, she probably won't be able to make nice with him over shrimp cocktail. Do your best to check for random relationships that may not be immediately apparent. One way to do this is to casually mention someone's name to one of your potential guests. If they respond with an "Oh, I can't stand that bastard, he fired me from my first job," you automatically know not to bring those two together. If Your Guy's friend Louis is the lawyer representing Mabel's ex hubby, don't sit them together. Don't even invite them to the same party.

MIXING IT UP

Gathering a great group starts with thinking about people you and Your Guy would want to sit next to at a dinner. Who to include? Your Guy's friend since age five, the cool actor who is about to make it big on Broadway? The wise and wickedly funny professor who lives across the hall? Your Guy's boss, Ronald, and his girlfriend, Crystal, a former Vegas showgirl rumored to have been a call girl? Only inviting people who have similar lives, similar jobs, and similar backgrounds will be dullsville. You both bring a wide variety of friends to your marriage, so a dinner party is a great time to bring them together. Toss in your friends from work with his friends from the gym. Mix people who have different political leanings, marital status, pedigrees, nine-to-five gigs, or hairlines. Don't forget the importance of having a few duds in there. Good listeners are valuable at a dinner party, otherwise you'll have a tableful of people who don't want to share the spotlight. So feel free to invite Olivia's geeky husband, Internet Guy; just seat him next to Ronald's lively girlfriend.

MUSICAL CHAIRS

Once the MG and Her Guy have selected a groovy group they should get down to the business of placing people in prime spots. Write everyone's name down on an index card and arrange your table by shuffling your cards around like a puzzle. First step, always separate couples. Otherwise, a shy husband will just cling to his wife's conversation, leaving out his dinner partner on the left. It also helps steer the conversation to more independent ventures. Second step, set people up. If Frank is looking for a job in the entertainment industry and Rita is the hottest agent in LA, sit them together. Same goes for potential love matches. Sitting singles together at a dinner party is a painless way to introduce potential soulmates. If they hit it off, you'll be toasting them at their wedding. If not, they can always chat with the person on their other side. Third, roll with it. Some dinner parties are going to be fantastic events where no one wants to go home and others are going to end with people racing for the door as soon as they inhale dessert.

Entertaining Without Spending Big Bucks

Stocks not going your way? You don't have to cut back on evenings with good friends just because you think it's too pricey. There are plenty of ways to host a good time without dropping too much moolah. Mrs. Impossibly Smug Married Girl may always have caviar and Cristal at her parties but that doesn't mean you have to. Most people are thrilled to be entertained and are just as happy to have burgers. If you want to make things feel fancier when serving inexpensive grub, serve it on your good china.

There are several easy and classy ways to cut down the cost of a dinner party. The obvious one is to have potluck suppers. Suzy brings a salad, Olivia makes dessert, Fred brings wine and all you have to do is provide a decent main course. Another cost cutter is selecting ingredients and foods that aren't that pricey and are in their prime. Choose chicken over ostrich and only buy asparagus when it's in season. Scheduling your dinner party around the farmers' market day or a trip to a wholesale club is a clever way to get bulk produce, booze, flowers, cheese, and sometimes fish at a fraction of the cost. Or just go mellow. Sunday night spaghetti dinners, with a choice of sauces and incredible garlic bread, are a cheap and fab option. For alcohol choose one drink for the night. Don't worry about stocking up on ten different types of liquor.

THE MG FILES:

Party of Four

Being total movie buffs, My Guy and I thought it would be a blast to host a little Oscar soiree at our place. We recruited eight folks ready to don some Harry Winston knockoffs and cast their votes on the big winners and losers of the night. My Guy and I were in party prep mode for the week. I made some delicious dip, whipped up a few desserts. My Guy printed out ballots, clipped Oscar predictions from the paper, made sure the tube wasn't on the fritz, and made a batch of mojitos. At this point we considered ourselves seasoned party throwers. I had thrown a thirtieth birthday bash for My Guy, a coed baby shower, a few wedding showers, several successful dinner parties, and thought I was prepared for everything. Well, almost.

The day came. People were supposed to show at 7 P.M. My Guy managed to sit through the red carpet hour with me and even offered his own commentary (too much emphasis on dresses, not enough on cleavage). What a guy! At 7:45 I noticed we had a message. Played it. "So sorry, but Oliver and I can't make it tonight. He's sick and I don't want to leave him home alone." OK, two down. A bummer, but no problem.

Two seconds later, the phone rings. Maybe it's Oliver calling to say he had a miraculous recovery and is gracing us with his presence and insider knowledge of Hollywood? No, not Oliver. It's my friend Allegra calling to say she has a terrible case of the stomach flu.

She would love to come but can't. I think, "But I have so much food and Oliver and Andrea just canceled! I have Pepto-Bismol." Then I realize that my thought has actually come out of my mouth. I apologize and attempt a more mature response. "Don't even think about it," I say. "There is nothing worse than going to a party when you're feeling sick." Allegra was potentially coming with her husband so that's two more down. We're down to six. "Cool, more sushi for me," says My Guy, who's not fazed by our incredible shrinking party.

8:15: Party of two enjoying Whoopie's monologue. Still just My Guy and me. Phone rings again. I don't want to answer it for fear of more no-shows. It's Sasha and David, he's finishing up the basketball game but they are on their way. Happy they aren't calling to bag. We don't care how late they are. 8:45: Sasha and David arrive and gamely fill out their ballots and put money in the pot. 9:00: My fabulous friend India arrives and tries to get revved up, but she's got a shoot at 6 A.M. and her guy got in late from a weekend away, so she can't linger. She kindly stays for about fifteen minutes. After she leaves it's four of us with a one-hundred-piece sushi platter, forty cookies, thirty brownies, countless crackers, too much dip, and a pitcher of mojitos.

Six people canceled, and nothing went according to plan. Disaster? Was the party over? No. We had a heated, very close race for the $40 we had in the pot (I lost). We enjoyed our mojitos, and ate an awful lot of sushi. Sasha and David actually stayed through till the very end. We had such a blast we resolved to meet again next year, same tube, same time.

Do Not Try This at Home:
Top Six Entertaining No-No's

DON'T SERVE DINNER AT 11 P.M.

People get cranky when they're hungry and have kicked back a few too many because cocktail hour has lasted for three hours. Serving dinner at 11 P.M., unless you're in Paris or Madrid, will most likely result in a bomb of an evening with bombed guests.

DON'T ASK "WHO THE HELL IS THAT?" ABOUT SOMEONE YOU DON'T KNOW AND DIDN'T INVITE

While you may have been psyched when a handsome stranger walked through your door when you were throwing a singleton gathering, now you may view uninvited guests with less excitement. If you see someone you don't know at your own party, introduce yourself and tell him you're glad he or she arrived. Don't mutter to Your Guy that you can't believe Olivia's husband brought that Mr. Random, act like you knew he was coming all along.

DON'T GET READY AT THE LAST MINUTE

Unless you make a point to shower and change about an hour and a half before your party gets started, you may not get a chance to lather up. If you're trying to finish everything before you get yourself into your little black dress, you'll never get there. You've got to put it all on hold and get yourself spiffed up, otherwise you'll be answering the door in your sticky apron. Also, you don't want to be hopping in the shower when you have guests in the other room. Unless you're at the Playboy mansion, there's something a little weird about being at a party while your host is naked in the next room.

DON'T EMBARRASS A DRUNK FRIEND MORE THAN THEY ARE ALREADY EMBARRASSING THEMSELVES

Olivia's a little tipsy. She's slurring an impassioned speech about saving the whales while standing on your couch. Hmmmm, guess she had too many Thoroughly Modern cocktails. If she stays any longer she's going to launch into a show tune or two. Be a great friend and get her hubby to fake a terrible migraine. She can blame him for being the party pooper instead of thinking she was ushered home because of her tipsy ways. If you try and tell a drunk person they need to go home, they'll only want to stay and prove they're not drunk. Better instead to put the blame on someone else and make Olivia the hero. Stuff a little Alka-Seltzer in her purse.

DON'T NOT ENJOY YOUR OWN PARTY

At some point in the evening you and Your Guy need to throw the worries out the window and invite the good times to come on in. If you don't have fun at your own party, what's the point of having one?

DON'T ASK IF YOUR FRIENDS ARE HAVING A GOOD TIME
They are. And if they're not, it has nothing to do with you. You've planned a spectacular event and it would be impossible for them not to appreciate it. Now get out there and circulate!

CHAPTER SIX

A Whole Lotta Lovin':
Keeping the Flame Lit Like a Torch

Imperfectly Ever After

He's perfect. He's dreamy. He's the ultimate man. He makes mad passionate love to you on demand and doesn't stop until you're exhausted, beyond satisfied, and taken to a higher plane. When it's over, he whispers how beautiful, gorgeous, and sexy you are. You spoon. He holds you all night long and doesn't complain about an arm cramp. His favorite thing in the world is to just kiss and he can make out happily for hours. He always sees your side of things and frequently says, "You're right! I never thought of it that way." He loves to do everything you do. He likes movies with subtitles, chick flicks with Meg Ryan, and anything dubbed a romantic comedy. He especially loves going shopping with you. He is happiest sitting for hours on an expensive boutique's couch missing Sunday sports and a football game in the park with the guys. When you spend fifteen minutes debating whether or not to buy something, he will encourage you to buy it, take your time, and try on *more* dresses.

He loves everyone in your life, even your mother, whom he constantly compliments and calls just to chat. He is the wittiest guy at a dinner party, and has everyone in stitches with his one-liners and colorful anecdotes. He never makes a bad financial move. He encourages you to spend freely and impulsively and never ever questions your purchases. His stock portfolio, job track, and bank account are always going UP. Fear is not in his vocabulary. Should a dragon or a rabid dog attack you, he would slay it with one hand. He would never run in the other direction screaming. There is no sport he is not a master of. Love handles and pot bellies aren't to be found on his incredible bod. You are never rendered sleepless from his tossing and turning, talking in his sleep, or snoring. He loves to communicate and will talk about his emotions or explore yours for hours. What he really wants to know is how you *feel*. When you are irrational, he soothes you, massages your feet, runs a bubble bath, makes tea, and buys you a gift certificate for a facial. Every once in a while he will rent a billboard just to say "I love you."

Huh? If you have a husband like that, can you give me his number?

The ideal husband, that ultimate man back there, is simply a figment of your single-girl imagination. That dream guy who matched your twenty-point list of what you conjured up when you were solo. The reality of life and marriage, however, is that you've probably landed a great guy who's imperfect (just like you) but incredibly *perfect for you*. One of the biggest challenges contemporary MGs face is to let go of the myth of a perfect husband and a perfect marriage. After all, you spent years waiting for not just the right guy, but your SOULMATE. You didn't *have* to get married so now that you are, you figure it better be damn incredible. Even the smartest MGs around get sucked into the fantasies that surround happily ever after.

The truth is that when you move from singledom to coupledom you're trading in one set of trials and tribulations for another. Both independence and partnership have their own unique complications. Sure, you're giving up awkward blind dates, men who make breaking hearts a professional sport, and the angst of wondering if you're ever going to find anyone. But with wedlock you're gaining a few stresses as well—making decisions with someone who may have a completely opposing viewpoint, the challenge of loving someone when the chips are down, and dealing with their cute and not so cute habits.

That's why "imperfectly ever after" is the mantra of a wise and happy MG. To have a happy marriage you have to stop putting pressure on yourselves to be some idealized glamour couple. Sure, he burps (even though you could swear he never did before you signed on the dotted line) and he can't dance, but he also makes you laugh so hard you sob and he knows just when to call you in the midst of a tough day. He even puts up with the fact that you cry at the drop of a hat, snore occasionally, and have no idea what a PE ratio is. Just like you, he's delightfully imperfect. Together you are an assortment of quirks and maybe even a few flaws. But it works beautifully. And that's what matters.

How to Make Your 1,023rd Date as Fantastic as the First

Before you're married, you long for the day when you two will have your own cozy place and unlimited time together. You never thought you'd be dying to get out of the house. Fact is, no matter how long you've been hitched you still need to date. That's right, get spiffed up and paint the town pink. Bring out the perfume, the matching lacy lingerie, and devote an evening to your amour. If after 1,022 dates you're out of ideas and resorting to popping on the tube and popping corn (yawn), you need to shake up the marriage tree.

Part of the excitement of dating was that you never knew what the night would have in store (karaoke, Cirque du Soleil, or a baseball game?). Your adventures made for tales to share with your friends and conversation fodder for you two. Keep that sense of surprise and plan a few entirely unexpected date nights to keep the flame lit like a torch. Here are a few ideas for an offbeat and memorable date night every Married Girl should have up her sleeve:

FEAR FACTOR

Try something completely out of the ordinary, completely out of character, and completely terrifying. Face your collective fears with some daredevil therapy. Afraid of taking the plunge into parenthood? Take sky diving lessons and you won't ever be scared to leap into something new again. Fear of drowning in debt? Go scuba diving and hunt for sunken treasure. Are you and Your Guy both terrified of giving up control? Go tandem hang gliding and you'll have to trust each other and steer your flight together.

DANCE FEVER

Sometimes you gotta dance the night away to get in the love groove. Beyond the box step you stumbled through at your wedding, it's always fun to add some new steps to your repertoire. For nights you're feeling sultry and sexy throw on a red dress, drink some sangria, and catch a live salsa band. In the mood to shake your thing? Bust-a-move at a hip-hop club. Your Guy hasn't danced since the seventies and doesn't want to embarrass himself in public? Throw on some bell-bottoms, part your hair in the middle, don your platforms, and spin some dynamite disco in your private living room.

DINING OUT

You two probably have a local restaurant where there's a table with your name on it. Branch out of your neighborhood hot spot and embark on a culinary tour of your city. No need to always do a three-course meal. If you're a fan of foie gras, comparison shop for the best in town. Or go on a dessert tour, trying a new bistro for crème brûlée one week and death by chocolate cake another. And don't neglect your special occasions restaurant—sometimes it's good to go for no special reason at all.

GET LOST

Check airline and travel websites for last-minute deals. On a Tuesday or Wednesday log on and see where you lovebirds can fly for cheap. Usually the best fares come with off-season destinations or random departure times. Don't let that stop you from renewing your vows in Vegas on Christmas, or cheering on the rodeo in Cody, Wyoming.

CHEAP DATE

If you don't have as much spending money as you'd like, it doesn't mean you're locked into staying at home. There are a million and two free date options. Grab a guidebook and take your own architectural tour of your town. Listen to an up and coming author give a reading at your local bookshop. Check out art galleries. Go to late nights at the museum. Lace up your sneaks, hop in the car, find a scenic spot and go for a run. Let him chase you again, just like old times.

THE MG FILES:

Get Out of the House

So here we were in a new town a few weeks into our marriage. Everything was great. Almost. My Guy got home for super late every night and our "dates" involved me cooking, him eating, and us falling asleep exhausted. I woke up one morning and decided that might be OK when we had babies and were chained to the apartment, but not now! My Guy came to the rescue with a city guidebook, and we made a vow to discover a new spot every week. He picked hiking up the tallest peak in the state and bowling, I chose ice-skating in the park and a French movie. It didn't matter if we caught the late show or last call, as long as we got some time out. So groovy to be dating again!

Hot Guys, Bombshell Secretaries, and Other Marriage Booby Traps

You're sailing along the road of marriage and THUD! CRASH! BAM! You run smack into a marriage booby trap—an awfully attractive diversion that could temporarily or permanently derail your marriage if you're not careful. The key to avoiding these booby traps is to know what to expect. Follow the Boy Scout motto and always be prepared.

HOT GUYS

You're on your way to meet Your Guy for an après-nine-to-five martini. You saddle up to the bar about fifteen minutes early, looking smashing. The bartender, a beyond-handsome specimen, asks what he can get for you. You lock eyes and you're trapped in his baby blue gaze. He is the hottest man you've ever laid eyes on. You stutter. You actually blush. You try and divert your eyes, his handsome mug is too much for your poor married eyes to take. . . .

You thought after you got hitched that you would never notice another man again. Your radar was turned off and all your attention focused on your adorable guy. But at some point, you're going to notice, even have a harmless crush on some hunky man. You'll realize that you and Your Guy aren't in some protective bubble where you never find anyone else attractive. It's a shock to the Married Girl, who just assumed that marriage creates an automatic barrier that blocks out hunky lotharios and sexy twenty-five-year-old girls from her married world. It can throw you off when some dashing man on the train strikes up a conversation or you notice that your painter looks just like Russell Crowe. The worst part is that these incidents often occur just when you're in a spat with Your Guy and his imperfections are currently outweighing his assets.

As long as you acknowledge that it's normal to notice that your waiter has some serious biceps, but it's not normal to want to touch them, then you're fine. An MG is a natural flirt but she knows where to draw the line. Smiling at a man who's taken with you is OK, slipping off your wedding band isn't.

You will also notice that whomever you do have a crush on is simply someone who represents whatever your husband is not being that week. If he's obsessing about work and paying no attention to you—an unemployed actor who has hours and hours to devote to you may seem awfully appealing. If he's cranky and serious today? A Conan O'Brien type will have you in stitches. If he's not communicating enough—Ari Fleischer's your man.

BOMBSHELL SECRETARIES

OK it's a cliché. His dental assistant, secretary, or the au pair next door is a total babe. But when an MG comes face to face with a gorgeous creature who is occupying Her Guy's time, she's ready to sharpen her claws. Of course this is the wrong way to handle this. You don't want The Babe saddling up to Your Guy cooing, "I think your wife is threatened by me." Instead, become The Babe's best buddy. Invite her out with the girls. If she's single, offer to set her up. Bond. Ask her what she's looking for in a guy. If she says that the single world is terrible and that you're very lucky to have landed such a perfect guy, tell her about Your Guy's flaws. Make things up. Tell her he has a serious problem with gas. Mention his hairy back. Point out all the eligible men around who don't have hairy backs. She doesn't need to know that Your Guy's back is muscle laden not hair laden.

No self-respecting woman could have a wild flirtation or a mad crush on her friend's man. So if The Babe is your gal pal you won't have anything to worry about. Now when it comes to women who have no self-respect, you'll just have to trust in Your Guy. The thing about men is that their radar never really turns off. But most men just see finding the opposite sex attractive as a normal fact of life and don't worry about it. Sure they think, "She's cute," but they move on. It's never, "She's a lot cuter than my wife."

The Other Man: Don't Even Bother

At some point during your marriage you may miss the thrill of first kisses, the chase, and infatuation. You may look across the bedroom at your husband and think, "Oh, him . . . Again?" You may reminisce about some sexy chemist with whom you had a lot of spark. You may fantasize about when you didn't know who you were going to be sleeping next to for the rest of your life. Any smart MG laughs this off as just a normal phase of monogamy that's not worth worrying about. Just rekindle the flame with a night of passion and then you'll be looking across the bedroom and saying, "Him! Again! Please!"

If you fall into the trap of thinking the grass is greener on the single side be advised that very few women run off and live in bliss after they've been an adulteress. You should know from watching enough Lifetime movies that affairs lead to heartache and courtroom scenes more than anything else. Here are the likely outcomes if you make the mistake of cheating:

YOUR GUY FINDS OUT

Your Guy finds out. He is heartbroken, horrified, and hell-bent. He kills your lover in a savage murder that is splashed all over the papers. Your Guy admits to the crime and goes to jail for life. Before he leaves he says he truly hates you, and looks at you with a venom in his eyes that you still have nightmares about. You get divorced. Your life is analyzed and debated on Fox News 24/7. Geraldo calls you a hussy and the ladies of *The View* agree. In jail Your Ex becomes best friends with a reputed mob boss. You are always looking over your shoulder for some Tony Soprano thug to take you out. Your Ex marries a surprisingly attractive woman who writes to him after seeing the story on *Inside Edition*. You are left alone, penniless and publicly embarrassed. No one trusts you anymore, because you lied to everyone to cover your tracks. You pose for *Playboy* because you are notorious and desperate for cash. You consider moving in with Hugh Hefner and his gal pals but Hugh says you're too old for him. Your family supports you, but spends most of their time writing to Your Ex-Guy in jail apologizing for raising a woman who cheats on a great guy.

YOUR GUY DOESN'T FIND OUT

After a night of torrid love with your secret beau, you return home. You feel horribly guilty every time Your Guy does anything nice or affectionate. Despite the nagging guilt, you continue to see your lover on the sly. After a few hot months, Casanova gets bored with you. The thrill was in the forbidden and you've been too available lately for Casanova's liking. He dumps you. He starts dating your single younger sister. You can't tell her to stay away from him because you can't reveal your affair. At parties you will have to watch them make out in the corner.

You have horrible nightmares that involve Your Guy finding out and confronting you about your sin. You start to go mad with guilt. You have to take serious antidepressants and you spend your days feeling like you're in a fog. The fact that your husband is the funniest, kindest, grooviest guy on the planet suddenly dawns on you. You can't enjoy it though, your secret is eating you alive. Your Guy cannot stand to be married to you anymore since you have completely changed and become a mopey, unpleasant, angry person. He reluctantly leaves you. Casanova marries your sister, they have five kids, and live lustily ever after.

So keep your conscience clean!

Privacy Please: The Bedroom Boogie

Fireworks! Sparks! Chemistry! A happy MG knows that sex is one of the most crucial parts of the love equation. Sex is surrounded in lots of myth and boasting so it's hard to know what's true and what's not about married sex. Here's the MG scoop behind a couple of the married sex myths:

SEX SLOWS DOWN AFTER THE HONEYMOON

If there's chemistry before the honeymoon there's going to be chemistry after. You're probably not going to be having crazed sex every day like when you were first discovering each other's bods, but you won't see a sudden drop-off either. More likely, you'll occasionally miss a week here and there, and start to panic. Don't. Some weeks you're hot, some weeks you're not, it's just life.

MARRIED SEX ISN'T AS PASSIONATE AS SINGLE SEX

There's some comfort in knowing what to expect from each other. But knowing *exactly* what to expect every time would make you prefer reading a good romance novel to rolling around in the sack. Luckily, sex, like marriage, is a work in progress. It's always changing. One thing is certain—married sex will be more passionate than the sex you had earlier in your life. It's more intimate, more powerful, more uninhibited, more open. After all, this is the man who's seen you at your best and at your worst. When you feel completely comfortable to let loose, you'll be surprised where you two end up.

SEXUAL READING:

An MG's Private Library

When an MG and her man want to add a few new moves to their repertoire they turn to the sexual gurus for inspiration. Whether you want to simply add some spark to your love life or become a sexual dynamo, these are the books you should go to for lust lessons:

The Art of Tantric Sex, **Nitya Lacroix**

Hey, if tantric sex works for Sting and Trudie, it can work for you. Sure it's a little different and requires a lot of time and a lot of patience, but devotees claim it's worth exploring.

The Kama Sutra

There are almost too many modern versions of this ancient Indian guide to sex, including a *Complete Idiot's Guide*. Even if you two think you know everything there is to know in the bedroom, this book will prove that you don't know the half of it. Pick a version with illustrations rather than the creepy posed and airbrushed photos.

Satisfaction: The Art of the Female Orgasm, **Kim Cattrall and Mark Levinson**

Tough to believe, but even though she's been married before Cattrall claims to have never had good sex until she met her current hubby, Mark Levinson. Hallelujah for Mark! This guy knows how to please a woman, and Cattrall seems like one very satisfied MG. Together they share some very handy tips told from both their perspectives. Very informative reading, for both you and Your Guy.

The Anniversary Party: Ways to Celebrate Your Marriage

Every year you have an opportunity to celebrate your good fortune in finding each other. Every year you also have to come up with a new way to commemorate your wedding vows. Here are some unexpected ways to toast your first five years:

FIRST ANNIVERSARY: DIVE IN

Last year you took the plunge into the unknown waters of wedlock figuratively. This time take it literally. Put on your finest swimwear and head to the beach, the pool, or the lake. Dive into the water hand-in-hand to celebrate your act of courage.

SECOND ANNIVERSARY: THE POWER OF TWO

Go two-stepping. Make a double chocolate fudge cake. Go tandem sky diving. Celebrate your good fortune of living life *à deux*.

THIRD ANNIVERSARY: BE NAUSEATINGLY IN LOVE

Celebrate with a PDA. Hire a sky writer or a personal fireworks display. Take out an ad in the personals. Be gushingly, disgustingly romantic and publicly declare your love for each other. It's always good to be a sap, especially on your anniversary.

FOURTH ANNIVERSARY: VEGAS, BABY, VEGAS

What bride didn't have fantasies of giving up the whole big party and hopping on a jet to Vegas? Hit the chapel to renew your vows, and this time wear leopard-print pants, toast with a shot of Jack Daniels, and give each other a juicy French kiss at the altar. Your real wedding was probably terrifically tasteful, here's your chance to be terribly tacky.

FIFTH ANNIVERSARY: PARTY CENTRAL

Have an anniversary party. Same guest list, same band, different outfit, new spot. Five years is your first big milestone on the road of marriage so make a fuss.

Never Surrender

Every MG worth her salt made sure she didn't say "love, honor, and obey" in her marriage vows but instead "love, honor, and cherish."

Who wants to obey anyone else anyway? You're not a dog, you're a wife. But a woman named Laura Doyle wrote a book for Married Girls advising them to change their independent ways and surrender to their husbands. A collective gasp was heard from Thoroughly Modern Married Girls across the land. In *The Surrendered Wife* she advises giving husbands the credit cards and letting them be in charge of everything. She advises never saying "I think" and instead saying "Whatever you think." This is her cure for her own marriage, which was unhappy because she was a controlling "shrew."

Don't believe the hype! There are a million books out there filled with bad advice. Of course it makes sense that if you are a controlling shrew your marriage will probably not be the happiest of unions. But becoming subservient and repressing your own opinions aren't the answer. Instead try being nicer, less controlling, and not assuming you're always right.

Married Girls know that equality in a marriage doesn't always work perfectly. What does work is when one person is a star at something, then, regardless of their gender, they're in charge of that. If you're the money genius and can make $500 into $5,000 with some clever investing, then you should take charge of the finances. If Your Guy is an amazing chef and loves nothing more than whipping up a splendid roast beef or some incredible gazpacho, then let the kitchen be his domain.

Another option is to surrender chores and tasks to the experts. If neither of you can balance a checkbook, check in with a financial advisor. Whatever you do, never surrender your power to each other. Your Guy would hate having to be in charge of everything. What a burden! Thoroughly Modern Guys prefer having a soulmate who's also a teammate.

Romance vs. Real Love

On *Oprah* recently a pretty blond woman stood up and lamented the lack of romance in her marriage. "But I thought marriage was going to be one big date," she said. The audience laughed.

Women who think marriage is going to be an extension of dating, with every night about romance and roses, have read too many novels with Fabio on the cover. Dating Your Guy is a must, but expecting married life to be one big date is wishful thinking.

Wedlock is about so much more than pink tulips and love notes (although those are very much appreciated). True love doesn't necessarily grow stronger because you've planned an evening of dining and dancing and staring at the stars. But love grows deeper during a million odd moments that can't be constructed out of champagne and caviar—when he holds your hand through a death in the family, or you help him get back in the ring on a day when he feels like quitting. In those moments when the image of perfection fades away and you're both vulnerable is when real love occurs, and it's not the chocolates and flowers kind. Hard to believe, but after you've gently applied calamine lotion to his terrible case of poison ivy or when he buys four different kinds of pregnancy tests just to be sure, you'll feel the bond between you cement itself.

Club Wed: Having a Blast Together

Me Time or We Time? Navigating Free Time

Now that you've got a partner in crime, do you do everything together? What if he doesn't share the same secret affection for attending live WWF events as you do? What if he spends every Saturday in the summer racing sailboats while you get seasick just standing on the dock? Do you stick like glue to your honey or take time out to pursue some hobbies solo? Now that you're married you'll have to figure out how to navigate your free time as a couple. Here are a few tips to ensure that your downtime keeps looking up:

LEARN ABOUT SOMETHING HE LOVES
(AND EXPECT HIM TO DO THE SAME)

Your Guy loves nothing more than to go to a good late-night jazz club and smoke a good cigar. You're nuts about horses and the rush of galloping at high speeds across rolling fields. Maybe you're not interested in jazz and he's terrified of horses, but take a stab and learn about a few things your partner loves other than you. He doesn't have to jump on a runaway horse, just visit the barn every once in a while. You don't have to sit through hours of jazz, just pick up some stogies and some Miles Davis CDs. You do have to be supportive and interested in each other's solo projects. If you don't take an interest in something that's got Your Guy excited or vice versa, you run the risk of living separate lives. Then you risk growing apart and one of you falling in love with someone who's passionate about the same stuff. And what Married Girl wants that? Not you.

LEAVE HIS SIDE EVERY ONCE IN A WHILE

Making Your Guy do every last thing with you will ultimately drive him to drink, heavily. Have you seen those poor husbands who get dragged into the nail salon? The sad fellows have to sit on a teensy, uncomfortable couch for an hour, next to some woman who's drying her pedicure and gossiping loudly about Julia Roberts. Then the guy is forced to drink herbal tea when he just wants a Coke, and read *Allure* when he really wants to read *Maxim*. Unless you're trying to torture your husband (if he's in the doghouse, this is a good way to do it) don't insist on doing everything on your to-do list as a pair. Your husband is not your girlfriend. Things your girlfriend loves to do or chat about may not hold the same fascination for Your Guy. While he's probably a terrific guy to be with most of the time, he isn't the ideal companion for every activity. For example, your friend Olivia will be a much better accomplice at a sample sale. She can elbow that girl who's trying to steal the last Gucci skirt, snag it for you, and honestly tell you if it makes your butt look huge. Your Guy would look at the sample sale experience in an entirely different light. He might complain endlessly about crowds, prices, and say things like "But you already have a black skirt." Doing things separately now and then allows you to enjoy things that you both love independently of one another. And smart MGs know that a little independence only enhances your together time.

FIND SOMETHING YOU BOTH LIKE TO DO TOGETHER

Hopefully this is an easy one. You never argue about how to spend your free time, because you have at least one or two hobbies in common. If you don't have any shared passions (outside of the bedroom) learn something new by taking a class together. Try something that you both haven't done before and experience the thrill or horror of it together. Bonus if you pick up something you'll use out of class like shiatsu massage to get the knots out of a hard day, foxtrot lessons so you can dance in the dark, or Surfing 101 for days you play hooky and hit the beach.

Don't Go Trying to Change Your Man: A Cautionary Tale

Soon into her marriage to the undeniably handsome, but slightly geeky, Internet Guy, Olivia made a common MG mistake, she tried to change her man. Olivia, like many brides, had overlooked a few of Her Guy's flaws hoping that she could wave her wifey wand and the magic of marriage would make them disappear. She was crazy about Internet Guy and didn't want to completely change him, just spruce him up a bit. Her goals for the Internet Guy makeover were to make him into more of a social stud and less of a computer stud. A few new clothes, new friends, new activities would do the trick. Now that he was her husband, Olivia saw him as a reflection of her, and she wanted to make sure he looked mighty good.

Olivia polled her married friends and found that their guys often met up on Saturdays and played golf. She was determined to get IG in with the golf guys. So on a Saturday afternoon when Internet Guy would normally be trying to sell his socks on eBay, or emailing *Star Trek* fans about episode 35, Olivia made arrangements for him to play a round of golf. Internet Guy really only liked socializing with Olivia or socializing with friends he met in chatrooms. He was not thrilled about spending time with Olivia's friends' husbands who wore plaid pants and only called him when their AOL wasn't working. So you can imagine IG's response when Olivia told him to get ready to tee off.

Only after lots of pestering, a great deal of pouting, and a potential sobfest did Olivia convince Internet Guy to go. He took off his Kiss T-shirt from 1975 and handed over his vintage Levi's. She outfitted him in a Polo Golf outfit, complete with plaid golf cap and gave him a golf-ball keychain for good luck.

The game was not a success. Frank, who he was teamed up with, was a sore loser and threw his clubs around after Internet Guy bungled not one but eighteen important shots. Afterward at the club, Internet Guy didn't have much to say. When talk turned to other sports like baseball, Internet Guy tried to pitch in. He knew the stats of most major league teams since he had a baseball section on his website. This helped a little, but the bottom line was Internet Guy just wanted to be home with Olivia, and the husbands just wanted to be on the green without him.

Internet Guy was normally an incredibly romantic guy who showered Olivia with amour but the following week he spent all his free time reading Tiger Woods' *How I Play Golf*. On Saturday, game day, after Olivia had ushered him out the door with his expensive new clubs, she logged on to his website, www.ralphlovesolivia.com, to read his daily love poems, and saw he hadn't written all week. Olivia realized Internet Guy had hardly been on his computer at all because of the golf lessons he'd taken every night to ensure that this game was less torturous than the last. Come to think of it, Olivia had been pretty lonely without Internet Guy at home. She decided she didn't like being a golf widow. Olivia wanted her old geeky homebound husband back!

Luckily, IG hadn't even dragged his feet out of the driveway. He was only too glad to be missed. They headed to the planetarium, hand in hand, and that night IG put his clubs up for sale on eBay.

Great Escapes: Vacation Ideas Under $200

So you blew your savings going first class to Bali for your honeymoon? It doesn't mean that you're confined to your pad for the rest of your vacation time. There are plenty of inexpensive and offbeat ways to escape. Here are a few Thoroughly Modern ideas:

LEAVE US ALONE! LOVE IN A HOTEL

Have you had enough of your boss calling at 10 P.M. to go over the numbers, your brother-in-law calling to "borrow" some bills, and Stan calling at 11P.M. to go out? Tired of that mountainous pile of dirty laundry and the disaster that is your kitchen? You need to escape your life and check into the love hotel. Check the Web for special rates, check the paper for ads, and check into an inexpensive room in your own private hotel island. Let someone else turn down your bed, put a chocolate on your pillow, and deal with your dry cleaning. Order burgers in bed, in-house movies, and put a little dent in the minibar. You don't have to leave your hotel all weekend. Lounge by the pool, run on the treadmill, and take a bubble bath for two. If you live in a small town, make sure to park your car around back. You wouldn't want anyone to find you.

HIT UP YOUR FRIENDS

Your buddies Lucy and Larry have a stylin' ski house? Your boss has a cool Colorado cabin that he never has time to use? Weasel an invitation from friends in nice places. If they're inviting you to join them, you're obliged to sing for your supper. Always arrive with a creative hostess gift (please, not another bottle of wine). For a house with a great porch, try a telescope, if your hosts live for their two dogs, bring up dog treats and some stylin' dog sweaters. Be flexible, helpful, don't have loud sex in their house (if they're there) and you'll be guaranteed an invite back.

THE DAY-TRIPPERS

Chances are the biggest expenses on your vacations are airfare and hotel. Eliminate both by choosing vacation spots that are within driving distance. Leave at seven and get back in time for *Saturday Night Live*. Whether you go to a theme park, or a historic house tour, make your day feel like a package vacation. Do some research and avoid the golden arches in favor of local hangouts and off-the-beaten-path places to get some grub. And don't forget to bring your camera, you're on vacation!

THE MG FILES:

The Things I Do for Love

I am standing at the top of a ridiculously steep ski trail in Vermont. I am avoiding looking down because each time I do, I feel a wave of panic and envision myself falling painfully down the entire mountain, breaking bones I didn't even know I had. Not only am I terrified, but I'm freezing. My eyes are tearing up from the cold, my nose is running, and my cheeks are stinging and bright red from windburn. Even worse, several young children are fearlessly whipping past me. Just as I am gearing up to attempt to ski, about ten people wipe out on a sneaky patch of ice that no one seems to know how to handle. A few skiers almost meet their maker when they have a near miss with an out of control snowboarder shouting, "Look out, Dude!" I want to turn around and ask the chairlift operator if I can ride back down on the lift. The toasty lodge with its leather club chairs and fireplaces is calling me. I look back down at the steep drop wondering, "How exactly did I get here? Did I actually pay money for this?"

I had imagined skiing would be a little more glamorous. I envisioned myself donning some sleek outfit and shimmying down a mountain like a Bond Girl. So when we were courting and My Guy first invited me to his ski share, I eagerly accepted. I ignored the fact that the last and only time I skied (thirteen years prior) I barely mastered the snowplow. I just figured it would be easy to pick up.

The first morning, the alarm rang at 6:45 A.M. (way too early for a Saturday). I sleepily put on my cashmere turtleneck, sunglasses, faux-fur earmuffs, and a black jumpsuit I borrowed from my sister. My Guy took one look at me and chuckled. He said, "You might be a little cold. It's five degrees outside." So he geared me up, handing me extra layers that added an unwanted twenty pounds. He lent me some goggles with orange lenses and a ratty wool hat with a red pom-pom that reminded me of the hats I sported at age eight. I topped the look off with a green fleece neck warmer I wore up to my eyes. Bond Girl I was not.

As we rode up the lift, I suggested the bunny trail. "What? I thought you had skied before," said My Guy, looking slightly nervous. "Well, I have skied before, but it was only once and it was in 1984." I honestly thought we had gone over this already. My Guy looked worried. He asked if I wanted a lesson. "Lesson? I don't need a lesson," I said as the chairlift got to the top. I stood up to get off, accidentally crossed my skis, and pitched forward into the snow.

Thankfully, My Guy used to be a ski instructor so he patiently taught me the basics. He's my security blanket on the slopes. He doesn't mind skiing on slow trails with me and never ever makes me do black diamonds, unless I want to, which I usually don't. Of course it's been a long process getting me from being flat on my face in the snow to attempting mogul runs in Montana. I once started down a trail My Guy swore wouldn't be difficult. I got about twenty yards down and felt duped. It was full of moguls and ice. Desperate, I took off my skies and climbed back up to the top. Another time, after sitting on a chairlift that didn't move for ten minutes in a blizzard, I shouted, "This is not my idea of a vacation!"

But somehow, after starting this whole skiing thing because it was something he loved and I loved everything about him, I actually dig it. A few months ago, I even took some runs on my own after he headed into the lodge for an après-ski beer. I see skiing as an exercise in facing my fears head on. Hey, if I can get down a trail without killing myself then I can do anything! Would I be skiing if My Guy didn't exist? Maybe not. But sometimes we do crazy things in the name of love. Even careen down narrow ski trails at warp speeds, wearing unattractive outfits with icicles hanging off our eyebrows.

Hectic Lives: What to Do When Time Is Not on Your Side

Husband? What husband? Sometimes schedules, unlike your love, are incompatible. What a bummer when you work from six to five and he clocks in a twelve-hour day that ends at nine. You schedule-crossed lovers only have about an hour together each night before you pass out. You're like vampire lovers who only interact after dark.

You thought being married was all about togetherness, but lately you spend more time with your dog than you do with Your Guy.

Since having fun together is an essential ingredient in the life of a Thoroughly Modern Married Girl, you've got to be crafty. So you don't have time, you do have some smarts. Here are a couple of MG solutions for hectic honeys:

MAKE AN APPOINTMENT

Call his lovely assistant (with whom you've made friends, of course) and book him for an hour's consultation under an assumed name, Madame Funn. This solution is easier if Your Guy is a therapist or a lawyer, harder if he's a construction worker. Then use your time wisely, sneak off for a stroll in the park or stroll to your bedroom. Whatever you do, celebrate that you're getting to see his cute mug in the daylight hours.

HAVE A PICNIC (IN THE OFFICE)

Even if you're up to your hairline in work, a girl's got to fuel up once in a while. If you can't go home to eat, let Your Guy bring the grub to you. Your Guy might offer you a hoagie from the place that doesn't deliver or fix your favorite salad Niçoise. You can now flirt with the delivery guy with abandon since you're married to him. While you may only have fifteen minutes before you have to dash off to make your deadline, you'll at least be able to say you had dinner together.

LOVE THAT EMAIL

Since you never know which corporate tech guys are reading your emails and you might by accident press "Send" to the whole company, sending dirty emails from work is not advised. But sending a little love note or some other romantic gesture, like a Web link to a picture of the beach you went to in St. Bart's, is just the thing to keep you connected when you're apart. The bonus is that because you're at your computer you'll appear to be working.

PLAY HOOKY

Sometimes you've got to both call in sick and then call a cab to the beach. While your careers are important, nothing is more important than your marriage. So take a vacation from work and clock in some hours together. On days you play hooky, it's got to be all about having a blast. Just don't go out to eat at your boss's favorite lunch spot.

CHAPTER EIGHT

Negotiations and Love Songs: Handling a Spat or Two

Diary of an Argument

With deadlines looming and deals being made, you've barely had time to say hello, much less be romantic. You've decided to remedy the situation and planned an elaborate lovefest of an evening that starts with a five-course dinner. You rushed out of work early, leaving a grumpy boss. You didn't expect to come home to a grumpy husband. You tried your hardest to ignore his foul mood and figured he'd snap out of it within minutes. You lined up votive candles in the center of the table, pulled out your antique silver, and put Ella and Frank on the stereo. You dusted off your cookbooks and actually boiled, baked, steamed, and stir-fried instead of your usual microwaving. You envisioned an evening of scintillating conversation and gourmet cuisine, followed by snuggling and an old movie. He envisioned an evening stewing over his bad day in front of ESPN, snuggling with his Bud.

Seeing the effort you've gone through brings Mr. Grouchy over to the table. He loosens up a little when he sees you've prepared lamb stew. You get a "Thanks!" But he's still cranky. You bring up a few subjects—the mummy exhibit at the museum, his friend Ed's thirtieth birthday party, the car show you just got tickets for. He doesn't respond but occasionally grants you a "mmmmm" in between mouthfuls. You suspect he's not listening. You test this theory out: "On my way to Saks, I was abducted by aliens." His response? "Mmmmmm." **Strike 1**. Now you're annoyed.

You want him to tell you what's wrong. No dice. All you get is this: lousy day, nothing to do with you, lost major account, need to think. You can respect that, right? Well, no. After all, one of the main reasons for marriage was to not be alone anymore, to be a team. You want him to share with you. You want to make it all better. You want to solve his problem, together. You want to *talk*. To him, talk is a four-letter word.

He mentions that he likes the lamb but asks why you don't cook this way every night. **Strike 2**. Now you're mad. You explain that you don't do this nightly because you also have a job and this type of cooking involves hours of shopping, chopping, and praying it all works out. You also mention that his being grumpy and uncommunicative doesn't inspire you to ever cook again. You ask why *he* doesn't cook five-course meals every day? He says he doesn't know why you're so touchy tonight. **Strike 3**. Now you're ready to fight.

You have two options here. You can follow the marriage advice of your minister and countless self-help gurus and Never Go To Bed Angry. Or follow the advice of wise Married Girls and Go To Bed Furious. If you try and duke it out before bed when you're both exhausted, chances are it will end badly. After a half hour of fighting you'll be no closer to a resolution but probably angrier. It's practically impossible to resolve a disagreement late at night. Things always seem ten trillion times more dramatic and less resolvable. Small issues seem like they're divorceworthy. Someone may end up sleeping on the couch.

Wise women let it go until the morning. They go to bed steamed, but find themselves waking up in their husband's arms. It's so hard to be annoyed when you're snuggling. In the dawn of a new day, everything somehow seems better. It's easier to put everything in perspective. Sometimes you even forget what you were annoyed about. Not convinced? Here's what to expect if you follow the old advice or if you follow the new, clever MG mantra:

SCENE 1: TRYING TO DUKE IT OUT BEFORE BED
(NEVER GO TO BED ANGRY)

11:05: Tell him in a firm but calm voice that you're mad, really mad. Look at clock. Explain why. After five minutes of explaining, stop. Ask him what he has to say for himself.

11:10: Apparently, he's got nothing to say for himself. Announces he's going to sleep. Mutters under his breath that you're a drama queen

11:12: Tell him he's a drama . . . king! (Lame comebacks always happen when you're exhausted) Tell him he can't go to bed without resolving what you're mad about. Ask him if he learned anything in premarital counseling. Don't wait for a response. Explain that if he did learn anything, he would know that you two should never go to bed angry.

11:15: Asks why he can't go to bed mad. Says he's totally capable of doing so. Promises to discuss this at length tomorrow. Says that you're only making him madder by keeping him awake.

11:18: Yell that he's making *you* angrier by not resolving the issue at hand. Tell him you also have to get up for work tomorrow. Start comparing whose job is more difficult and requires more sleep.

11:19: He sits up. Wants to know why you think your job is more difficult. Asks why, if your job is tougher, do you make less money.

11:20: Rant about misogynist pigs who devalue woman's work.

Don't remind him that your boss and CEO are women. Emphatically state that you should get paid twice as much as he does.

11:22: He mutters something unpleasant under his breath, he's pretty peeved.

11:23: You don't have a comeback. Desperate, bring up the time he was rude to your best friend, Olivia. Bring up the time he drank too much at the office Christmas party.

11:25: He has no response for this. Looks furious.

11:27: Go back to why you're mad at him tonight, and why you were mad at him last week. Realize you are having the same argument you had last week, last month, and possibly last year.

11:30: He lists off several grievances to counter your claims. The one he seems most annoyed about is that he had to watch the *Today* show when he really wanted to watch CNBC.

11:33: Realizing that this doesn't make you feel sorry, he recalls another sore spot. He brings up the time you maxed out the credit card at the Barneys warehouse sale.

11:40: Explain you were buying things for HIM at the Barney's warehouse sale. Lie and tell him you thought he really liked the *Today* show.

11:45: More yelling. Tears. A pillow gets thrown. So does a blanket.

11:47: He moves to the couch. He says keeping him awake to argue is a form of torture.

11:48: Alone and in bed you debate whether or not to apologize.

11:50: Alone on the couch he debates whether or not to apologize.

11:51: You both decide never to apologize.

11:52: Exhausted, you both fall asleep.

SCENE 2: WAITING TO DUKE IT OUT IN THE A.M.

(GO TO BED FURIOUS)

11:05: Crawl into bed. Don't say anything. Wonder if he even notices how mad you are.

11:10: He crawls into bed with you. You are still steamed so you move over to the other side of the bed. You don't want to be near him.

11:12: He is oblivious to the fact that you're angry. He moves over to your side of the bed. He puts his arms around you. Try and move over, realize that there's nowhere to go but the floor. Decide to give in and sleep in his arms.

11:15: Exhausted, you fall asleep

2:15 A.M.: More snuggling.

7:05 A.M.: Wake up

7:06: Oh, right. You were mad last night

7:08: Why?

7:10: Your Guy is in a good mood. Sweet. Kisses you. Apologizes for being so grumpy. Seems to want to talk about his feelings.

7:15: Decide to forget about it and forgive him. Maybe you'll mention it later if you still think it's worth talking about. You don't say anything. Just hug him.

7:20: Move on to smooching. Decide it's OK to be a little late for work . . .

Love Conquers All, Even a Dumb Disagreement

Of course, now I can't remember for a second what we were arguing about. But we were in the midst of having a huge spat. The kind of spat where one of us says, "SHHHH, the neighbors are going to hear us," and the other one gets even louder and shouts, "I don't care if the neighbors hear us!!!" (Of course the next day we pray the neighbors didn't hear anything.) Neither of us wanted to back down. I wasn't going to be happy until he agreed with me, until he apologized profusely, until he told me I was right.

Was he going to say he was sorry? No. He thought I was wrong, extremely wrong and that I owed him an apology. He had the nerve to tell me I was being irrational. I didn't take to that very well. My response was to yell, "Well I don't want to stay here with someone who thinks I'm irrational! I'm leaving!!!" I stormed over to the closet and pulled out my overnight bag. As soon as I had my overnight bag out I felt silly. Where on earth would I go? It was five below zero outside.

I looked over to see his reaction. Was he terribly upset that I was going to be leaving? Was he rushing to my side to beg me to stay? No. He was calm. Not even the slightest bit perturbed, worried, or concerned. In fact he had moved to the bed and was calmly reading. He looked as if he could fall asleep at any moment. My Guy wasn't going to have any part of my childish antics. This made me so irritated that I continued packing. I wanted him to be terribly up-

set about the thought of my being so upset that I would pack up and leave. I thought maybe he would say he was sorry.

Nope.

I walked out the door. I was, of course, acting like a thoroughly unmodern MG (not to mention uncool). Once outside, I put my ear up to the door hoping to hear him rushing after me. Instead, I heard him turn on the hockey game. I went downstairs and turned on the car. Maybe he would apologize if he saw me get into the car! I sat in the car with my overnight bag filled with a random assortment of items I had thrown in there. I think I had packed a cocktail dress and a pair of running shoes. I thought about driving away just so he could see me driving away. Then he would apologize! But pretty much all I could think of was how incredibly stupid it was to be arguing when we could be having a fun night. There wasn't anywhere I wanted to go except back home.

After about two minutes my cell phone rang. It was him. "Yes?" I answered. "I thought you would want to know your favorite movie is on TV," he said. I waited for him to apologize. Nothing. He told me the score of the hockey game. Then he laughed and joked, "I know you're sitting in the car around the corner. I thought I would call you to give you a chance to say you're sorry." We both laughed and I headed back upstairs, where he was waiting with a huge grin on his face and open arms.

There's no place like home.

Ground Rules

You're going to have spats, tiffs, and occasional knock-down-drag-out brawls. It's part of living, loving, and making major and minor life decisions with another person. It's not the part of wedlock that you dreamed about, but it's a fact of married life. Since you know that at some point, you two are going to disagree, set some ground rules. While most of your arguments should be fairly painless, when you're in the heat of the moment sometimes people do crazy things. Don't be one of those couples who think throwing pots and pans, throwing tantrums, and hurling insults means you're "passionate." Instead fight with a little class. Here are some basic ground rules that will ensure that you two can make up, not break up, at the end of a spat:

DON'T FIGHT IN PUBLIC

OK, sometimes your timing stinks. You'll be out at a party wanting to hit the hay but Your Guy will be ordering another round pretending not to notice. "You never think of me," you hiss just as your best friends arrive to chat. Everyone freezes and you look like a shrew.

There's nothing more embarrassing than fighting in front of other people. It presents an unflattering portrait of your marriage and makes everyone feel extremely uncomfortable. If you are constantly bickering or trying to bring other people into your arguments, people will start avoiding you two. If you're the type of woman who thought flinging her chardonnay in your boyfriend's face at a party was an effective way to make a point, you now have to find less dramatic ways to communicate when your husband makes you mad. When you two don't see eye to eye when you're in the public eye, have some codes. A wink may mean "Let's discuss this at home later." Touching your ear might mean "I'm miffed but I'm going to let it go because we're in public." Two winks may mean "Pack it in, we're going to settle this outside." Be prepared. Your Guy may think it's funny to pretend he doesn't know what your codes mean. He may just laugh and ask if there's something in your eye.

DON'T BRING UP THE PAST

In the midst of a disagreement, it may seem like a good idea to bring in past examples of his bad behavior to bolster your case. Don't bring up the speeding tickets he hid from you, the bonus money he lost playing the slots, or the time he skipped your mother's birthday party. You've already argued about these things before and he's probably apologized a million times. Instead when you present your side, stick to the issue at hand. When you bring up Your Guy's every blunder, things just go from bad to worse. He'll tune out your point entirely and you'll find yourself having the same old argument instead of resolving your current dilemma.

DON'T TAKE OFF

We all get the urge to flee the scene when things get hairy (see "Love Conquers All" above). We want to lace up our Nikes, run out of the apartment, and never look back. Frankly, sometimes it seems a lot easier to drive off into the sunset than deal with your standoff. This, however, only sends a message to Your Guy that you're going to bail when things go wrong. Checking into a hotel, or staying at your mother's, is unnecessarily dramatic and it brings other innocent people into your quarrel. The last thing you want is your mother or your best friend worried, when all that's happened is you've blown a silly spat out of proportion. Leave the divalike behavior behind when you get hitched. If you absolutely have to have a change of scenery, take a walk around the block (but tell him where you're headed). Staying put will also force you two to come to some sort of resolution that you can live with.

DON'T SAY THINGS YOU CAN'T TAKE BACK

At some point during an argument it is going to occur to you that you can say or do anything, because now that you're married he won't break up with you. This of course is flawed logic because if you repeatedly throw hissy fits, or say nasty things, you create a tear in your marriage that becomes increasingly hard to sew up. After you make up it's hard to be loving with someone who not a day before called you an idiot. Not every zinger your brain conjures up needs to be verbalized. If you have a problem with blurting out insults in the heat of the moment, take a time-out before you state your case (or try passing notes).

DON'T LIE

Some people think lying is a clever way to get out of things. But one little lie tends to lead to another. Soon you'll be telling lies to cover other lies and you won't be able to keep up with yourself. So fess up. Did you go skydiving when you promised to be less of a daredevil? You've got to come clean. Never expect a make-out session because you told the truth. Telling the truth can be unpleasant, but it's got to be done. If you aren't both completely honest with each other, especially in those moments when you know you won't get caught, your relationship will suffer. You'll be constantly suspecting each other of lying or worse. If you can't trust each other, what's the point? Your marriage should be a safe space, not a place you rummage through each other's desks in search of proof of wrongdoing. If you want to do that kind of snooping become a private investigator.

Attracting Bees with Honey

Those Southern belles know what they're talking about. Throwing in a "sugar" or "sweetie pie" or my favorite, "darlin'," into a conversation instantly makes Your Guy lighten up and listen up. If you've got something you need discussed, something you want changed, something you need done, don't bitch him out. Instead, sidle up to him, rub his shoulders, throw a few "lovies" his way. Tell him five great things he's done and he'll be much more apt to listen to the one bad thing you need to discuss. Nagging sometimes works but being your sweet self always does the trick. Make Your Guy feel like a stud and he'll act like one. Make him feel like he's failing you and he will inevitably disappoint you.

Truth or Fiction?

Don't believe women who tell you they never fight with their men. It's not possible, it's not healthy, and it's just not true. Everyone argues, whether it's minor bickering or serious disagreements. Some couples shout at the top of their lungs while others dole out the silent treatment. In interviewing brides for this book, I noticed that women I didn't know well were always eager to paint their marriages perfectly pink. My good friends, however, were quick to share a laugh about a recent spat. When casually interviewing a lovely young Mrs. at a party, the topic turned to arguing styles. What was hers, I wanted to know. She looked me right in the eye and said, "Oh, Gerald and I never fight. I can't remember the last time we had a fight. It's been at least a year . . ." Her Guy was standing nearby and overheard the tales she was spinning. Laughing, he interrupted with, "What are you talking about? We fight every day! We had a fight ten minutes ago! You just said I was an idiot." His bride proceeded to blush. Flabbergasted, she tried to save face. She told me he was just kidding while flashing him some serious deadly glances. The "yearly" fight was about to begin.

Four Surefire Ways to Make Up

Making up is the best part, in fact, it's the only good part of fight-ing. When you want to give Your Guy a kiss rather than the silent treatment, you need some ways to smooth things over. Here are a few ideas so you can stop fighting and start loving:

ACTUALLY SAY "I'M SORRY"

In *Love Story* Ali MacGraw tearfully pronounced that "love means never having to say you're sorry." Most Married Girls will tell you otherwise. Sometimes sorry goes an awfully long way toward mak-ing things right. Sometimes love means only having to say you're sorry, then everything gets dropped, forgiven, and left in the scrap heap of battles never to be fought again.

TAKE OFF ALL YOUR CLOTHES, JUMP INTO BED, AND SUGGEST MAKE-UP SEX

When all else fails never underestimate the power of transferring anger into hot sex. Your juices are flowing already so you may as well get out your aggressions between the sheets. Ideally, when it's all over you won't remember what you were arguing about, or one of you will be happy to cave in.

BAKE

They say the way to a man's heart is through his stomach. Whether or not you believe that old wives' wisdom, inject your best brownies or your killer apple pie to at least stop his noise. If his mouth is full because he's devouring your peanut butter squares, he can't possibly argue with you.

RAISE A WHITE FLAG

Agreeing to disagree may save you a lot of energy. Sometimes you just have to accept that you're never going to see eye to eye about certain subjects. He's always going to think your sister is a flake. He's always going to sleep in and you're always going to wake up with the birds. There are some things you're never going to change about each other. Hey, if Mary Matalin and James Carville can stay in love despite their extreme political differences then you two can too.

CHAPTER NINE

Money Matters: Merging Your Finances Without Separating

Great Expectations

It all starts with registering. One second you're living with two mis-matched placemats and a hand-me-down set of beer mugs from your older sister. Then the next second you're standing in Bergdorf's picking out French china patterns with a price tag equal to half your rent. Registering is so magical, isn't it? You enter your favorite shops, point to whatever you want, and a few months later, voila! the items appear on your doorstep. It throws off your sense of reality and sets into motion a chain reaction that has you pointing to houses, cars, rare dog breeds, designer clothes, boats, and jewels you also covet, and dreaming that POOF! they will all be yours just a few months later. Hey, it worked before.

After "I do," great expectations suddenly appear, demanding they be met and not even your plastic can keep up. As a sassy single you may have been happy in a slightly run-down apartment sporting the same pair of versatile black pants four times a week. But add a hus-band to the list, a top-notch ceremony, a first-class honeymoon and you'll want a spiffy pad to show off your new French china, your new guy, and your new outfits. You want to be grown-ups, and grown-ups have cash. Throw Your Guy's own expectations into the mix, and you're headed for heartbreak city. Just because you're married doesn't mean you've become different people with different bank balances (although that might be nice). Smart MGs and their men learn to keep their expectations reality based. It might be years be-fore you move out of your little rental. Things all happen in their own time. Remember when you turned twenty-nine and wanted Your Guy to show up already? Well, your Prince Charming arrived, not on schedule, but just at the right time. The same goes for all your material expectations.

Why You Can't Spend Your Last $60 on a Facial Anymore

When you were on your own you only had to answer to yourself and the landlord. As long as you were OK with the consequences you could be as impractical or as smart about money as you wanted to be. Felt like blowing your grocery money on a facial, and surviving on ramen noodles and canned tuna for the week? You gave that plan the green light. Felt like putting 30 percent of your paycheck into a Roth IRA? That plan got the green light too. You could invest in environmentally sound mutual funds or you could buy controversial tobacco stocks—it was all up to you.

Then Your Guy entered the financial picture and things got a little crowded. Your most personal financial decisions—"Should I move to a bigger apartment or should I stay put in my shack?"—aren't personal anymore. They involve someone else. Like most men, Your Guy thinks facials are ridiculous and would gag on ramen noodles by the third day of the week. Married life means taking Your Guy into account, and maybe even into your checking account.

Joint Checking Accounts and Other Scary Steps

Remember those months when you were single, and an unexpected expense, like car repairs or a bridesmaid dress, could wipe out your budget and you were left eating from free buffets at Happy Hour until you got paid again? Those were the months you wished for dollars from heaven, a raise, a good lottery ticket, or a second check in your checking account. Miracle of miracles! Now that you're hitched, there just may be that extra check. You have a few options for how you handle your money as a couple, and here are the ins and outs:

OPTION 1: WHAT'S YOURS IS MINE

You pool your hard-earned money and make decisions as a team. It's a good exercise in working together and so rewarding when you accomplish shared goals. The lovely fat sum of your combined income will seem like enough to cover basics *and* save for future dreams like a country house, two kids, or a trip to Morocco. Unfortunately, joint checking accounts don't always live up to their airbrushed fantasy. First of all, you're completely trusting Your Guy and he's totally trusting you not take all the rent money and blow it on a sports car or a night at the blackjack table. Second, when you're sharing a check register, you're going to have to account for where your money goes. Expenses you think of as essential, like pedicures, private karate lessons, and $90 underwear, he may think are frivolous. Same goes for him—his $2,000 kayak might not be where you wanted to spend your bonus. You'll find that you are spending a disconcerting amount of time talking about money—maybe even more than you talk about whose turn it is to do the dishes. This kind of money talk isn't fun and you'll soon understand why you're always hearing that money matters are the biggest cause of dreaded divorce.

A Thoroughly Modern Married Girl doesn't want to spend her time bickering over a few lousy dollars. The answer is for you and Your Guy to have a weekly or monthly money pow-wow to set goals, make budgets in advance of spending, go over your portfolio, and strategize on how to get where you both want to be. But bottom line, joint checking is a great option only if you two see eye to eye on long-term goals *and* life's little luxuries. If you're still a little rusty in the negotiation department, you might try the next approach.

OPTION 2: WHAT'S YOURS IS MINE AND WHAT'S MINE IS MINE

One clever solution to the joint checking standoff is for both of you to contribute to a joint account that covers household expenses and long-term savings, but also maintain your own separate accounts for your personal money management. The joint account is subject to negotiation, even bickering, but the solo account is yours to fritter or squirrel away just as you please. For a Thoroughly Modern MG who's been answering only to herself and AmEx for years, this may be the only dignified option.

OPTION 3: WHAT'S YOURS IS YOURS AND
WHAT'S MINE IS MINE

Have you ever been out with couples who scrupulously split the check, each paying his or her own share with their own funds? This could be a couple for whom pooling money resulted in one too many battles for control of the checkbook. Maybe one partner was too controlling, maybe one was seriously irresponsible, and their angst-free solution is separate accounts. This could also be a couple who hasn't really gotten with the notion that marriage is a team sport. Whatever the reason, this is no way to run a household economy. Unless you were both star savers as singletons, you'll find that it is harder to reach a shared financial goal when you don't have to account for how you spend your money. It's a lot easier to splurge on a $200 facial or a $500 handbag when you don't have anyone to report to, which has its pros and cons. It's great to feel like your money is your own, but there's nothing more frustrating than feeling like you can't afford to go to your friend's wedding in Paris because one of you hasn't saved at all.

ONE HOUSE, TWO STANDARDS OF LIVING

Option 1 sets you two up to divide things fifty-fifty. One account, equal access. Options 2 and 3 are trickier. It's doubtful that you and Your Guy make exactly the same salary, so if you're going to have separate accounts, does that mean one of you has more to spend? Nope. The Thoroughly Modern Married Girl is not interested in keeping Her Guy a vassal even if he earns like a serf. No matter who brings home the big bucks, you two have equal say in how it gets spent. If you keep joint and separate accounts (option 2), make them separate but equal. It's ridiculous for two people to live together with different standards of living. This is another reason why option 3 is really not an option.

Living Large on a Budget: Ways to Save a Buck or Two

Can you live large on a budget? Absolutely. You have to be a little craftier, but that's not a problem for a Thoroughly Modern Married Girl. Here are a few ideas for saving your hard-earned dough:

GO SHOPPING IN YOUR CLOSET

Your closet is often the best and first place you should go shopping. When you think you need a new dress for New Year's, first check out everything on the Home Shopping Network. Maybe that sleek navy strapless bridesmaid's dress just needs a little hike in the hemline to become the perfect cocktail dress. Or you just might rediscover that fabulous black pantsuit you had forgotten about.

HOST A POTLUCK PARTY

No need to hide from your friends because dinners out are burning a hole in your wallet. Instead, host a potluck cocktail party (everyone brings their favorite drink) or a potluck supper (everyone brings their favorite dish) and you've hit on an inexpensive way to entertain. Bonus: this should result in return invitations that keep you dining out for weekends to come.

TAKE A VACATION IN YOUR APARTMENT

Put your computer (email), pager, and cell phone in the basement. Turn off the ringer on your phone. Hide your car in the lot down the street and don't answer the door. Stash your bills and any work in a drawer. Ignore your laundry and any room that needs to be cleaned. Take a weekend getaway in your own place. Catch up on sleep, sex, and snuggling and shut out the rest of the pesky world, the way you do when you jet off to a hotspot. You might not have a beachfront view, but you don't have to pay the bill when it's over.

SAY NO

Invited to all the hot benefits in town at $300 a plate? Included in a girl's spa day outing for $200 a person? Expected to attend an anniversary dinner at the toniest restaurant around? While all of this sounds like an absolutely divine way to spend some time and some dough, if you're on a budget you've got to be comfortable saying no every once in a while. You don't have to give money as the reason for your absence, just claim a previous engagement or a family affair that you simply cannot miss.

Careening Careers

If you're like most MGs, your marriage probably hasn't made much of a change in your and Your Guy's ever-upward climb to fame and fortune. You got back from the honeymoon, showed up at work on Monday, and picked up where you left off before those blissful days in Bermuda. But a couple of common scenarios can make you realize that on the job front, it's not the same game as when you were single.

WHEN ONE OF YOUR CAREERS REQUIRES A MOVE

You're both plugging along in the big city trying to claw your way to the top, or at least up another rung. You just got a promotion and are thrilled that you no longer are expected to answer someone else's phone, pick up their dry cleaning, and take courses in filing. Your voice actually matters now and when you pitch an idea even your CEO responds. Your Guy is also hitting his stride after years of 10 P.M. dinners and schmoozing sleazy clients. You both love your careers, have five-year plans for where you want to go, and thrive on having even the slightest bit of power. Then the unthinkable happens. You get an amazing offer in the middle of nowhere for double your current salary and a hell of a lot more than his. How do you make this decision?

Well, of course you're going to think about the money. How badly do you need it and how quickly can it help you make your other dreams come true? Then you factor in the job. Is it a position that only exists in one place? Is it the dream job of all dream jobs? Then factor in his career. Can he stay on track if you move or is he taking himself out of the game? You also have to weigh the personal happiness factor. Is this job worth giving up your friends, family, and hip restaurants for life in the land of the nine-month winter? If after all that talking, you guys BOTH want to go, then pack your bags. The key is that even though it's your job, the decision affects both of you. You will both have to make compromises for each other, and the question every time is whether this is a compromise you both can live with.

HE HATES HIS JOB

He's making big bucks to launch you two into a new tax bracket, but he's miserable. He was raised to believe that work is work and fun is fun and you don't mix the two. But what he really wants to do is teach. He tries to grin and bear it, but he can't deal with the bear market and he's becoming a curmudgeon at age thirty-two. What do you do?

This is not a tough one. When it's money and misery vs. happiness and the unknown, take the unknown every time. You might have heard this bit of wisdom: Do what you love and the money will follow. How true. And it is also true that when Your Guy does what he loves, he will love you even better.

THE MG FILES:

The Marriage of Two Financial Personalities

I'm a spender. When money comes into my hands it doesn't stay there long. When I was single I had quite a load of credit card debt because I was such a short-term thinker, e.g., "I have an interview, I need a new suit!" or "I have a date, I need new perfume." Then I met My Guy, who is a saver, an investor, and a planner. Could a fly-by-the-seat-of-my-pants kind of gal find money harmony with a man who started saving for retirement at seventeen?

For me, being married to a saver opened my eyes. My Guy didn't preach, he just gave me the facts about compound interest: if you put x amount aside and invest at y percent, then you would have big fat Z in only a matter of time. It seemed crazy that I had never run the numbers myself, and I was abashed, but it still wasn't enough to make me change my spendthrift ways. Then My Guy did the math on the down payment of a little house we could own some-day and big fat Z took on new meaning. I was hooked. From that day forward I started a little house fund and now I put 20 percent of my earnings in the pot before it even hits the checking account.

Has this leopard changed her spots? Hardly. My natural instincts are still tuned in to the sample sale frequency. But now they pick up the real estate channel as well. If you're like me, it's not enough to save just for the sake of watching money grow. You need a goal— a white picket fence, a second car, a year off, or a trip around the world—and your shopping instincts and your saving muscle can work in tandem.

A GIRL'S GUIDE TO FINANCES
BEFORE AND AFTER "I DO"

Before you get hitched your money is your own. You can live pay-check-to-paycheck and rack up the Visa bills without a care in the world. You live for the moment, and sometimes the moment is just screaming for new shoes. But after the nuptials it's not just about you. It's about the two of you, your future, and saving for it. Cut up the credit cards, girls.

Before "I Do"

No money? No problem! Visa to the rescue.

Save for fabulous party shoes. Save for fabulous strapless dress to go with party shoes.

Shop for clothes, makeup, baubles, shoes.

Love showing off decadent new splurges.

After "I Do"

No money? No house. Cut Visa up into little pieces.

Save for house, save for baby, save for baby's college, save for retirement.

Shop for linens, towels, fabric, curtains, china.

Sometimes hide new splurges, especially if they're decadent.

Before "I Do"

Extra cash? Lipstick, magazines, manicures, shoes.

Never spend money on groceries, eat at cocktail parties, at business lunches, and dates.

Read *New York Times* and *Vogue*.

Keep an eye on fashion trends.

Role model: Holly Golightly.

After "I Do"

Extra cash? 401(k).

No more free dates, his money is your money. Discover eating in by candlelight. Bonus if your husband cooks (or at least microwaves).

Read *New York Times*, *Vogue*, *Wall Street Journal*, and *Forbes*.

Keep an eye on stock trends.

Role model: Suze Orman.

The Thoroughly Modern Married Girl's Ten Commandments

The Thoroughly Modern Married Girl's
Ten Commandments

You've gotten your financial house in order, thrown your first successful shindig, and learned the trick to making up after a spat. Now here's a little refresher course: the ten commandments to staying sensational after saying "I do."

1. Thou Shalt Not Live in a Bubble

Sometimes love is such a whirlwind of crazy joy that you forget that there are other people, things, and activities in the world besides the two of you. While this is understandable, you have to have outlets, otherwise you'll drive each other bonkers. Before you met Your Guy, you were always getting together with your gaggle of female friends, hanging out with your family, putting in extra time at the office, saving the world at the local shelter, or taking a few classes to keep expanding your brain. Don't stop. Just because you are Mr. and Mrs. So-and-So doesn't mean you have to be attached at the hip and forget about everything else. Your marriage will be a lot more interesting if you keep on being the fascinating gal you were before he met you. You'll also have a lot more to talk about over dinner.

2. Thou Shalt Respect All Forms of Life, Not Just Married Life

Life becomes awfully narrow when your social life revolves exclusively around other couples. One too many brunches spent talking about the real estate market will make you think you've died and gone to married hell. One benefit of your wedding was that you had the chance to introduce all of your previously separate social circles to one another. So once you're wed, keep mixing things up: his friends and your friends, work friends and school friends, neighbors and family, old friends and brand-new acquaintances, singletons and smug marrieds, parents of twins and the child-free.

3. Don't Worry. You've Still Got It

When you were single, you met cute guys everywhere—at the Laundromat, on the subway, at funerals. Once you're hitched, it's easy to miss the buzz of universal male admiring attention. But unless you're a movie star and you absolutely have to look lustily at other men because it's your job, don't go batting those eyelashes at anyone but your beloved. Don't worry, you still have the power. You've just got to take it on faith instead of soliciting daily proof.

4. Honor thy Mother-in-Law and Father-in-Law

Your in-laws may be incredible bores, gossipy and nosy, or so tacky and embarrassing you want to hide under your turtleneck when you're out with them. Whatever type you've inherited, welcome them with open arms whenever you see them. No matter what you think of them, remember that they are responsible for raising your terrific husband. Even if you really believe that he only turned out normal due to some sort of divine intervention (think Marilyn on *The Munsters*), give them the credit. So listen to your father-in-law drone on and on about weird weather patterns and act riveted. Eat your mother-in-law's scary meatloaf (even if you prefer things green) and don't forget to ask for seconds. Grab another glass of wine if necessary.

5. Thou Shalt Not Even Bother Trying to Keep Up with the Joneses

Let's get things straight. There will always be a couple that is funnier, more attractive, sexier, wealthier, nicer, hipper, healthier, smarter, more successful, and more glamorous than you two. Got it? Even if you are the grooviest couple in the room at one party, you won't be at the next. If you are constantly comparing yourself to other couples (some of whom you will find out later were just faking it on the road to divorce court), you will miss out on enjoying how happy you are just being yourselves.

6. Fight a Clean Fight

When you were dating and you got into a spat you may have found that slamming doors, crying, and racing back to your apartment were effective tools in winning an argument. He would be so lost without you that he would come running over and say he was sorry. Well, I hate to break it to you, but that tactic is not going to work now that you are married and living together. You're a lot better off staying calm and staying put to solve a tiff. Fight a clean fight and you are guaranteed at least that he'll listen to your point of view. Winning is up to you.

7. Be a Team

While you are both successful, independent people, don't forget to cheer each other on, support each other's crazy dreams, and encourage each other to live your best lives. If he's up for a promotion, become best friends with his boss at the office Christmas party. If he's always wanted to ride in the Tour de France, buy two tickets to Paris to see it up close. Lousy day for him? Treat him and his buddies to an after-work gripe session at the corner pub. On the days where your star is shining and his isn't, make sure to pass him the winning shot. In a mean and crazy world isn't it nice to know you always have someone on your side?

8. Be Fabulous

Be comfortable being unconventional, glamorous, or unique. You don't have to become June Cleaver now that you're hitched. Who cares if you guys like to have the Christmas ornaments up in June, don't have matching silverware, or prefer Pabst Blue Ribbon to a fine vintage? Let your hair down. You've found someone who loves you, warts and all, so be the marvelous offbeat woman that he fell in love with and never try to be some cookie-cutter Mrs.

9. Be Romantic

Sounds crazy but sometimes it's easy to forget what got you married in the first place. Don't stop being romantic, sexy, creative, impulsive, spontaneous, and crazy in love now that it seems easier to rent a video and order takeout. Take tango lessons, get season tickets to the ballet or hockey, go ice-skating hand-in-hand, and let him pick you up for a date. Don't be afraid to be unabashedly Hallmark-card cheesy and profess your love. Whatever it was that got you thinking he was the man for you, keep doing it. Most important, don't ever forget the power of an unexpected drop-everything smooch.

10. Be Thankful for Your Guy

There are times when married life will make you think back to your sensational single days with longing and alarm. You were Mary Tyler Moore, for God's sake, what made you think you wanted to be Edith Bunker? When the love of your life is driving you bananas, it is time to remember how sexy/suave/smart/sensitive/studly your man was the night you first decided that he was IT. Remember how lucky you are to have someone who puts up with all of *your* nonsense. If through everything, you remember to be grateful for landing the most wonderful man on the planet, your marriage will reflect that, every day.

Acknowledgments

Thanks to the many people who made this book possible: my hip and savvy agent, Neeti Madan, for believing in me; my brilliant editor, Kris Puopolo, for her marvelous ideas and editing wizardry; Monica Lind for creating a very glamorous MG; great Beth Haymaker and Sarah Walsh for helping the MG on her way to print; Robin Arnold for her terrific photos; the folks at Broadway for making this process so enjoyable.

I am extremely grateful to witty and wise MGs for giving me the scoop on navigating married life with finesse: Louisa McCall, Ashley Cole, Courtney McGinnis, Christina Lavallee, Alyssa Greenberg, Laura Campfield, Courtney Dann, Jessy Knoble Gray, Megan Schmidt, Elissa Kovas, Hadley Pollet, Jenny Gooch, Sarah Cody, Sanny Warner, Robin Taylor, Nina McKinnon, Julia Cahill, Liz Kuhse, Amanda Reynal, Kirke Hall, Casey Hamblett, and Kris Puopolo. With special thanks to entertaining goddess Emily Webster for her party tips and fabulous Allison O'Neil for her clever ideas and generous reading of countless pages. Thanks to my sassy sisters Jackie, Alyssa, Laura, and Cassie for their love and enthusiasm. Thanks to my wonderful parents for giving me a shining example of a thoroughly modern marriage.

Finally, all my love and endless gratitude to my hilarious and hunky husband, Brooks, for making me one incredibly blissful MG.

Sara Bliss is a freelance writer based in Boston. Her magazine articles on style, design, relationships, travel, food, and shopping have appeared in *Cosmopolitan*, *Boston* magazine, *House Beautiful*, and *Country Living*. Her first book on interior design, *Exotic Style*, was published in March 2002 by Rockport Books.